WORLD FAMOUS
GANGSTERS

WORLD FAMOUS
GANGSTERS

Ian Schott

|| **PARRAGON** ||

This edition published and distributed by
Parragon Book Service Ltd, Bristol 1996

Produced by Magpie Books, 1996
First published 1994 by Magpie Books
an imprint of Robinson Publishing, London
Copyright © 1994 Robinson Publishing
Illustrations and cover pictures © Popperfoto

ISBN 0 75251 773 2

British Library Cataloguing-in-Publication Data
A catalogue record for this book is available
from the British Library

10 9 8 7 6 5 4 3 2 1

Printed and bound in the E.C.

CONTENTS

Chapter One

THE SICILIAN DONS

Sicily is a parched, mountainous and pitiless country. Despite its small size, it possesses a peculiar sense of remoteness; it is full of wild, empty places, for hundreds of years the haunt of the infamous Sicilian bandits (these, often mafiosi on the run, were still customarily holding up vehicles in the 1960s). Apart from one or two cities favoured by the tourists, the morose and introverted island is covered by dull, crumbling towns, into which the rural population has traditionally huddled for mutual protection from the elements and from brigands.

It is an innately feudal society, and though the Sicilian princes and their houses have passed away, the Mafia has long since filled that power vacuum, and the Mafia dons have bought up the estates of the impotent aristocrats.

No one knows where the name "Mafia" originates. Sicilians say that when Sicily was occupied by the French in 1282, a young Sicilian woman was raped by a French soldier on her wedding day. Her distraught mother ran through the streets shouting *"Ma fia! Ma fia!"* (my daughter, my daughter). The Sicilians immediately rose up and massacred their French oppressors. It is also said that the name "Mafia" derives from a similar word in Arabic, which means "place of refuge".

But the Mafia, the very existence of which has been frequently denied, not only by its members but by prominent politicians, has been an integral part of southern Italian culture for centuries. For two thousand years the peasants of Sicily and southern Italy struggled against bitter poverty, rapacious landlords, and endured constant changes

When the Italians emigrated to America, the men of honour went with them, and were initially a useful defence against an often hostile American society. They protected the Italian communities, ran the lotteries, dealt with the authorities and offered loans. The Italians were ambivalent about the Mafia, or, as it was also known, *amici nostri*, meaning "our friends" (*cosa nostra*, another branch of the Mafia, literally means "the things we have in common"). They venerated these paternal criminals, while praying that their children would never enter into this strange, violent world, the detritus of which they would come across in the shape of unrecognizable corpses strewn over the local wastelands. Many families noticed, when burying some aged and withered relative, how heavy the coffin was. They would know that alongside their grandmother in the coffin lay some victim of a Mafia dispute, whom the undertaker had been asked to squeeze in.

of master as a consequence of territorial battles between princes; Sicily has been invaded no less than six times.

It was an anarchistic world, in need of order. But the law was the oppressor of the peasants, not their defence. As a consequence, a system of underground government evolved, run by men outside the law. These were often violent and committed criminals, but to the peasants their word was their bond, and they could be expected to arbitrate in local disputes, protect the people from outside marauders, preserve the integrity of the local culture and intercede with the nominal rulers of the land. Such a man, who had to be strong enough to avenge any insult to himself and his friends, took the title of *un uomo d'onore*, a man of honour, or *un uomo di rispetto*, a man of respect. They became the Mafia, the most closed and ruthless of secret societies.

Though the Mafia has long been driven by the pursuit of wealth, it has continued to rely for its support on this tradition of "honour". In addition, certain traits in the Sicilian character make it wholly suited to the temperament required of mafiosi. As an isolated race, the Sicilians have clung to the ties of blood and soil with a savage ferocity, in a fashion both atavistic and tribal; indeed some of their customs are echoed in the remote tribes of Africa and Asia.

The Sicilian tradition of the *vendetta* – a fight to the death between clans until honour is satisfied – is a mainstay of the Mafia mentality. Vendettas have made for some of the bloodiest episodes in the island's history. The worst vendetta of them all took place in the neighbourhood of the poor, dusty towns of Bagheria and Monreale between 1872 and 1878.

The two Mafia clans involved were the Fratuzzi and the Stoppaglieri, who were both active in the same area but had hitherto kept hostilities to a minimum. Then, in 1872, Giuseppe Lipari, a member of the Fratuzzi clan, committed what in Mafia parlance is called *infamità* by denouncing a member of the Stoppaglieri to the police. The Stoppaglieri duly sent word to the Fratuzzi that they should, in time honoured fashion, execute Lipari. This they failed to do, and a vendetta was born. Within months all the close relations of the original disputants had been killed, and the more remote kin were being compelled to participate in the tit-for-tat murders. When everybody who was officially a Fratuzzi or a Stoppaglieri was dead, the entire population began fearfully rummaging through its ancestry to find out if they too had some distant blood links which would compel them to participate in the round of killings. Within a

Gangsters

They say that there is nothing personal about a proper Mafia execution. These are the words of Nick Gentile, an American mafioso from Sicily, discussing the ethics of eliminating an uncontrollable young hood from his native country: "There was nothing we could do about him so he had to be rubbed out. We embalmed the body and sent it back to his people in Sicily. His folks were poor – they didn't have anything – so we put a diamond ring on his finger, the way they'd see it the moment they opened the casket. I guess we did the right thing. We figured otherwise that he'd end up in the electric chair or the gas chamber. That way they wouldn't even get his body back." The Sicilians regard the retrieval of the body after a murder to be of the greatest importance. For vengeance must be sworn "in the presence of the corpse". If the body cannot be found, the anger of the relatives has no ritual outlet. Hence the most perfidious of crimes are kidnappings in which the victim disappears altogether.

few years, a man walking down the street would find himself approached by a withered old crone swathed in black mourning who would inform him that he might not be aware, but he was now the surviving head of the Fratuzzi or Stoppaglieri clan, and was therefore in state of ritual vendetta.

In vain, many distant relatives of the decimated clans tried to emigrate, or conceal themselves; the area was becoming depopulated and reverting to wilderness. But the inheritors of the vendetta were always tracked down

Even in this century, some towns have been decimated by prolonged vendettas. The Mafia stronghold of Corleone, a tiny sullen town set in an unforgiving rocky landscape, experienced no less than 153 murders in the years between 1944 and 1948. Most of the bodies were never recovered. The town of Favara suffered 150 Mafia-vendetta killings in a single year; between 1914 and 1924 only one male inhabitant died of natural causes in old age (residents were not sure whether to be proud or not of this absurd statistic). Mass emigration to escape involvement in vendettas resulted in Sicily losing one-tenth of its adult population between 1953 and 1961; some towns became virtually uninhabited.

and forced to continue the feud, though the original ground for it had long since been forgotten. By 1878, the supply of able-bodied men was almost exhausted, and boys were being pressed into service. On one occasion a child was informed that in the absence of living seniors, he was now a clan leader, and, presented with a loaded blunderbuss, he was escorted to a point where he might attempt an ambush.

In the end, one of the few surviving Fratuzzi, a man called Salvatore D'Amico, who had lost all his family and was sick of the slaughter, offered his own life to end it. He went to the police and, in a repetition of the events that sparked the feud, informed on the Stoppaglieri, thus giving his own clan a ritual means to end the vendetta. The Fratuzzi understood D'Amico's noble intent; this time they made no mistake and duly killed him, displaying his body so that the Stoppaglieri might see that after six years and the blood of several hundred people the infamità had finally been paid for. Thus the vendetta was halted.

Another tradition of the Sicilian Mafia is that of *omertà*. Omertà is a complex notion. At one level it simply means "manliness", but at another it is to do with silence and self-restraint. When the police would come across a seriously wounded mafioso and ask him to identify his attacker, the reply would traditionally be couched in the followed terms: "If I die, may God forgive me, as I forgive the one who did this. If I manage to pull through, I know how to settle my own accounts." Such a response displays omertà. If wronged, a true man of honour will not wreak his vengeance in a rash, bloody act, or betray his anger; he will certainly not tell the authorities. Instead he will wait, for years if necessary, to avenge himself in the coldest way possible, often striking when he seems to be on excellent terms with the man he intends to destroy.

Although it stands outside Christian morality, the uncorrupted form of the feudal Mafia that survives in Sicily has a strict morality of its own. Mafiosi don't see themselves as petty criminals, but as lawgivers; they do not steal from the community, but take what is rightfully theirs in return for offering their continued protection. Killing is a pragmatic and at times inevitable action; a punishment.

The position of strength that the Mafia has achieved in this century, as it progressed from a federation of outlaws into a consolidated money-making machine, is largely the work of two formidable dons: Don Vito Cascio Ferro and Don Calogero Vizzini. These men struck the deals that brought the Mafia out of the shadows into the abandoned palaces of Sicily's lost aristocrats, and into the town halls.

In the early part of the century, Don Vito Cascio Ferro was for twenty-five years the undisputed master of Sicily. In his youth he had emigrated to America, where he had become a leader of the "Black Hand", an amalgamation of fugitive mafiosi and members of the Naples-based *Camorra*. While in America, he picked up a taste for smart expensive clothes and on his return to Sicily sported dashing, anachronistic garb: frock coat, wide-brimmed fedora, pleated shirt and flowing cravat. While other Mafia dons still dressed like surly peasants, Don Vito cut a sartorial swath through Sicilian society. He became an honoured guest at the salons of Palermo, opened exhibitions, romped with Dukes and Duchesses, frequented theatres, bought himself a phonograph and even took a hot-air balloon flight to demonstrate his interest in scientific advancement. Society women trembled with a strange passion when they spoke his name, and Don Vito had to reprimand his barber severely for selling off his hair cuttings as sacred amulets.

In the eighteenth century it was the Mafia, casting itself as a supporter of the popular leader Garibaldi, that whipped up the Sicilians into the violent frenzy that finally broke the shackles of the Bourbon state. When, before the turn of the century, democratic elections were held in Sicily, the Mafia took control of the political machinery and gradually drew apart from the people, blatantly compelling them at gunpoint to elect the Mafia's own chosen creatures. With political power assured, Don Vito was free to develop the system of *pizzi*. *Pizzo* refers to the beak of a small bird, and Don Vito adopted this term as a euphemism for racketeering, describing Mafia tolls and levies as "wetting the beak" – taking his cut.

Don Vito organized beak-wetting at the expense of the farmers, whose produce the Mafia bought dirt cheap and then sold at vast profits in the markets (where only those who had paid a levy were allowed to own a stall, and all prices were fixed by the Mafia). The Mafia also wet its beak in the meat, beer, and fish industries; in the sulphur mines, salt mines, building industry and cemeteries. It also took up a large portion of the tobacco smuggling racket and

Some of the rackets Don Vito established were quite fantastic. The Mafia imposed a tax on lovers, so that a young man going to court a girl who sat – as was the custom – behind a barred window, had to pay what was known as "the price of a candle" to guarantee his safety. The Mafia also exploited the financial opportunities offered by religion. It controlled the standing committees of the various cults of the Sicilian saints (the committees had access to the funds raised in the saint's name), and had a virtual monopoly on the manufacture of devotional candles. Later the organization began manufacturing religious artifacts, producing holy statues, medallions and even relics by the thousand; one Italian newspaper reported that there were in existence seventeen embalmed arms attributed to St Andrew, thirteen to St Stephen and twelve to St Philip. There were also no less than sixty fingers said to belong to St John the Baptist and forty "Heads of St Julian". All these had been manufactured and sold by the Sicilian Mafia, who discovered a vast market for these bogus relics in the United States. In areas where there was no saint and no holy relic to be prostituted, a convenient "miracle" would be arranged – the appearance of the Madonna to a child for example – to bring the pilgrims flocking in, who would buy their passage on Mafia-run coaches and stay in Mafia-owned guesthouses. The cult of Padre Pio, the "stigmatized" monk of San Giovanni Rotondo, who supposedly bore wounds similar to Christ's,

was one such scam. The Mafia created this
peculiar attraction, and fleeced the faithful, who
journeyed hundreds of miles to see this monk,
of a fortune. It even sold acres of bandages
asserting that they were soaked in the monk's
miraculous blood (in 1960 it was analysed and
revealed to be the blood of chickens).

cornered the market in stolen Roman artifacts. The owners
of country houses and estates were invited to employ
mafiosi as guards against the otherwise inevitable arson
attack. The Mafia sold and managed the monopolies in
every area of trade; even beggars were obliged to pay for
their right to occupy a prominent pitch.

The Mafia effectively replaced the police force as the
arbiters of law and order and thereby established one of its
most consistent sources of income: the recovery of stolen
property. If a horse, mule, jewel or, latterly, motor-car was
stolen, the victim would be approached by a mafioso who
would offer to recover the lost object for a commission of
up to thirty-three per cent of its value. If the commission
was agreed upon, the object would be virtually guaranteed
to reappear without delay. The original thief would be
compelled to sell the object back to the mafioso at a small
price (but would be grateful to escape with his life) and the
mafioso would profit at the expense of both parties. It was a
popular service; the police charged nothing but could only
recover stolen property in one case out of ten. The Mafia
might be expensive, but was successful ninety per cent of
the time.

This happy state of affairs continued until Mussolini
and the Fascists came to power. Although the Mafia
had contributed to the Fascists' funds (an insurance
policy; besides, Fascism was preferable to any form of

Gangsters

Communism), Mussolini was wholly distrustful of the
Mafia, realizing that its members habitually turned on
their allies. More importantly, the power of the Mafia
presented a direct challenge to the arrogance of his
authority. Il Duce made a most unhappy trip to Sicily
in 1924. He saw that the Fascist administrators were
powerless in the face of the Mafia, that the police could
obtain no witnesses to any crime, and that the Mafia-
elected deputies to Parliament devoted their time
exclusively to composing speeches denying the existence of their criminal masters.

On a tour of the island, Mussolini suddenly announced
that he wished to visit the grubby town of Piana dei Greci,
then run by a Mafia potentate named Don Ciccio Cuccia —
an ugly man noted for his acute vanity. Since it was an
unscheduled visit, the police had no time to make elaborate
security arrangements, and they realized that the only
guarantee of Mussolini's safety was to suggest that he
ride in Don Ciccio's car. When Mussolini sat next to Don
Ciccio, with the police motorcycle escort lined up on either
side, Ciccio turned to Il Duce and asked him why he was
bothering to surround himself with police; "Nothing to
worry about so long as you're with me . . ." he gloated. It
was then that Mussolini understood that he had no power
in Sicily.

On his return to Italy, the furious Mussolini immediately
declared war on the Mafia and assigned Prefect Cesare Mori
to the task of extermination. Mori was a stupid, pompous
and cruel man. Given *carte blanche*, he measured success
solely in terms of numbers arrested and confessions
extracted; his onslaught naturally provided an unprecedented opportunity for the settling of old clan feuds.
Hundreds of anonymous denunciations poured in; thousands were arrested on the basis of rumour and vindictive
gossip and shipped off to penal colonies. Mori would
frequently descend on a village and arrest the whole male

population. After a while, the people worked out that the only way of pacifying this vain monster was to erect a banner on his approach to the village, bearing the words "HAIL CAESAR".

In 1927, Mussolini proudly announced to the Fascist Parliament that his heroic colleague, Prefect Mori, had won the battle against the Mafia. In reality, it had been a bloody but ineffectual campaign. Most of the important "Men of Honour" had either made their escape or gone underground, or disguised their loyalties by joining the Fascist Party; they would be back. But at least many of the Mafia dons had been deprived of their quasi-feudal authority, and for the next few years — until the Allied invasion of Sicily — the peasants were better off than they had ever been.

One Man of Honour that Mori had managed to arrest was Don Vito Cascio Ferro. Charged with smuggling (on bogus evidence), the old don spent most of his trial disdainfully ignoring the proceedings of the court, becoming animated only when his defence counsel pleaded for leniency. "That," barked Don Vito, "is in conflict with my principles and offensive to my authority."

Prefect Mori reintroduced the use of the *cassetta*, a traditional tool of the Inquisition, to extort confessions. A small, low-standing box, it was used as a platform across which a torture victim could be painfully spread-eagled. Brine was then poured over his body and he was scourged; if he failed to confess, he was then forced to drink gallons of sea-water. Next his fingernails would be removed, then slivers of skin. If he still persisted in claiming innocence, his genitals would be crushed.

Asked if he had anything to say before he was sentenced, Don Vito stood up and, after carefully considering his position, said: "Gentlemen, since you have been unable to obtain proof of any of my numerous crimes, you have been reduced to condemning me for the only one I have never committed."

He had indeed over the years been charged with sixty-nine major crimes, twenty of which were killings, but no case was ever sustained. He only ever admitted to one murder, that of Jack Petrosino, an American detective whose researches into the Mafia had brought him to Italy in 1909. Don Vito, dining one evening with an influential politician, suddenly announced that he had to return home to attend to an important matter. He would borrow the politician's carriage and return immediately. He was driven into Palermo where he shot Petrosino, and then returned to his dinner. The politician happily swore that Don Vito had never left his house.

Locked up in the Ucciardone prison, Don Vito was the most beneficent of men, preoccupying himself with the welfare of his fellow inmates, who made his bed and cleaned his cell (thereafter something of a shrine, and only given to prisoners of equal honour). He even hired and fired the prison warders. He did not complete his sentence, but died of a heart attack. His death made Don Calogero Vizzini the acknowledged head of the Mafia and it was "Don Calò" who would engineer its resurgence.

The son of a peasant farmer, Calogero Vizzini was born in the small, shabby Sicilian town of Villalba in 1877. His family had some prestige locally, not only because they had the rare distinction of owning a few grim acres of barren land, but because Calogero's uncle was a bishop, and his brother the parish priest of Villalba — important considerations in a place where the church shares power with the police and the Mafia.

Young Calò was not a good student, and remained an illiterate all his life, perversely flaunting his ignorance and parochial bigotry. His first brush with the law came at the age of seventeen, when he was charged, unsuccessfully, with criminal assault. It seems that he took a fancy to the pretty daughter of a neighbouring family, the Solazzo clan. Though he had no intention of marrying her, he nonetheless forbade her to have dealings with any other man. When his honour in this affair was threatened by the girl's association with a rising young magistrate, Calogero and his gang burst in on the courting couple and beat the unfortunate suitor senseless. He nearly died, and the girl remained a spinster all her life.

At eighteen, Calogero went into business escorting grain shipments from peasant farmers across the remote, bandit-infested countryside to the flour mills. He did well, having struck a bargain with one of the most notorious of Sicilian bandits, Paolo Varsalona, who ran an extremely elusive band of brigands. Far from living their lives as roaming outlaws and making themselves an identifiable prey for the authorities, Varsalona's men maintained the outward appearance of respectability; they lived in the towns and pursued the traditional lives of peasants. At his call they would assemble, commit whatever crime was on the agenda, and then melt back into the workaday world. Calogero was so impressed with the bandit that he spent a number of formative years in Varsalona's gang, before they were finally caught in a police trap. Calogero was acquitted of murder on the grounds of "insufficiency of proof", and having made a sufficient impression on the necessary figures, was formally invited to become a member of the "Honoured Society" – the Mafia.

At the age of twenty-five, Calogero took the title of *zu*, meaning "uncle", and by the outbreak of the First World War was head of the Mafia in the Province of Caltanissetta. During the war he made a fortune from selling broken-winded and clapped out nags to the Italian cavalry; he also charged the farmers of his region to guarantee that their fit horses were not requisitioned.

Shortly afterwards, faced with claims that the army had become the country's largest receiver of stolen goods, the Italian authorities sought to put Calogero on trial. His inevitable acquittal brought him further prestige as the scope of his enormous influence was seen; he was allowed to take the title of "don" and so became, after Don Vito Cascio, the second most important member of the Sicilian Mafia.

When Mori's purges took place, Don Calò (as he was universally known) was sentenced to five years, but he had fostered good relations with a young Fascist administrator, and was quietly released a few days after he entered prison.

The years between Mori and the Allied landings in Sicily were a time of retrenchment for the Mafia. But from the early days of the Second World War, it was clear to the Mafia that there was much to be gained from co-operating with the Americans and the British. Firstly, the eviction of Mussolini and the end of domination by Rome (many mafiosi dreamed of Sicily becoming, if not an independent state, then a colony of the US or Britain); and secondly, the suppression of Communism, which threatened the feudal stranglehold of the Mafia. Furthermore, an invasion and the ensuing power vacuum would provide the necessary opportunity for the Mafia to reassert itself. Indeed, it was to be expected that the Allies would need the services of the Mafia, and would willingly make concessions in return for assistance in taking first Sicily, then Italy itself.

The full history of the Allied involvement with the Mafia has never been disclosed, but that it happened is no secret. Sadly, in some ways it is the US that is responsible for the dreadful Mafia rule that has so traumatized postwar Italy.

It seems fairly certain that the initial connection was made through the don of all dons, "Lucky" Luciano, who was imprisoned in America at the outbreak of the Second World War. He was released at the cessation of hostilities and deported to Italy, and it is believed that the price of his release was that the Mafia assist the American authorities in a number of areas. One such area was the surveillance of suspected Nazi agents and insurgents in America's docks, another was the invasion of Sicily. From Luciano the message was passed to Don Calò, and it all came to pass as planned.

When, on 10 July 1943, the Allies landed on the south coast of Sicily and began to push northwards, their forces were divided into two bodies. The British and Canadian troops ploughed up the east coast – in theory the easier invasion route – and encountered a poorly equipped and inexperienced enemy who nevertheless fought back well, compelling the battle-hardened British troops to a tough, five-week campaign. The Americans, on the other hand, were allocated the mountainous terrain of central and western Sicily, which appeared on paper to be a much more arduous task. Surprisingly, they obtained their objectives at startling speed, reaching the north coast with barely a casualty.

The key point in the Italo-German defence of the route was a series of fortified positions near the towns of Villalba and Mussomeli, commanding the route along which the Americans had to come. Here, under the command of Colonel Salemi, a man noted for his courage, the Italians and Germans gathered together a substantial force of artillery, tanks, anti-tank guns and foot soldiers. Though Salemi had no illusions as to the probable outcome of any battle, he knew that, given the strength of his position, he would make the Americans fight a long and bloody battle; he might be able to halt their advance for weeks.

But Villalba, as one will recall, was the home town of Don Calò, the beloved Mafia potentate of all Sicily. A few days after the Allies landed, American planes could be seen dropping strange packages into the town, which, it was later disclosed by a man who saw Don Calò unwrap one, contained yellow silk handkerchiefs embroidered with the letter "L". This stood for Luciano. It was a pre-arranged signal. On 20 July three American tanks made a dash into Villalba, flying yellow handkerchiefs, and bore away the invaluable Don Calò, who then went to join the US Army as guide and passport to bloodless conquest. It is reported that the meeting between the Americans and the don took place in utter silence; he knew precisely what the agreement was.

The following morning, Colonel Salemi awoke to discover that two-thirds of his troops had deserted. They had been approached in the night by mafiosi who had courteously informed them of the hopelessness of their position and given them civilian clothes in which to escape. Salemi himself was them ambushed and held in the Town Hall of Mussomeli by the Mafia. The Americans strolled through without firing a shot. Don Calò returned to Villalba to be greeted by cries of "Long live the Allies; long live the Mafia!". He was elected Mayor of the town and was thereafter accompanied by a guard of "anti-fascists" armed by special permission of the Allied Military Government.

He subsequently cornered the trade in olive oil, and divided his time between this lucrative area of the black market and controlling the post-war direction of Sicilian politics. The fall of the Fascists brought thirty-two alternative political parties into existence; the Mafia threw its weight behind the Separatist Party (later it would consider the Christian Democrats most suitable for its purpose). Don Calò considered it absolutely necessary that all left-wing parties be suppressed. When the socialist Popular Front asked permission to hold a rally in Villalba, they were most surprised to find the don warm to the idea. On 16 September 1944, as Girolamo Li Causi, the left-wing leader, began to address the crowd gathered in the town square of Villalba, the Mafia opened fire and wounded Li Causi and thirteen others.

Worse was to come. In 1945, the Separatists decided that an armed rising was necessary to guarantee their power, so Don Calò brokered a deal between them and the most famous of all Sicilian bandits, Salvatore Giuliano, who for many years had opposed the Mafia, but was to end up as its pliant tool. Giuliano offered, for a large sum, to attack the carabinieri outposts and precipitate the anarchy necessary for an uprising. But the Separatists had big plans: they raised a volunteer force, and dispatched it to join up with the bandits. Under Giuliano's command, this force was to await the chosen moment and then commence all-out insurgency. The order never came. Eventually the bandits left the volunteer army, which dwindled to fifty-eight men. The volunteers were then attacked by Italian military forces (sanctioned by the Allies) of 5000 men accompanied by tanks and artillery. It was an extraordinary battle. The Separatists were dug-in on a hill, and their assailants, though out-numbering them fifty to one, exhibited the most remarkable caution. The fight went on for over a day, and apocalyptic reports of it filled the press. When it was over, each side had lost only six men and most of the surviving Separatists had escaped.

Don Calò abandoned his support for the lost Separatist cause, but Giuliano continued to rage around the countryside, well equipped with weapons and explosives of American origin, shooting, robbing and blowing up all non-patriotic elements. The authorities made no serious effort to eliminate him: he was too useful a loose cannon. His violence had the effect of quelling peasant unrest.

Gangsters

Giuliano's moment of infamy came on 1 May 1947, the day of the elections to the Regional Parliament. Sicily was to be allowed independent status within the Italian state, and, since the Separatist movement was now defunct, the Church, the landlords, the Mafia and the Allies put their weight behind the Christian Democrats; the other parties supported the principle of land-reform, and were therefore considered dangerously left-wing.

For decades the people of the neighbouring towns of Piana dei Greci and San Giuseppe Jato had held a rally on May Day, at the mountain pass of Porta della Finestra. Quite apart from any political significance, it was a holiday, and the feast of Santa Crocefissa. But despite the Mafia's warnings, there was an increasingly upbeat Communist movement among the peasants, and they wound their way to the high mountain pass in a cheerful mood, singing and waving banners. It was a brilliant, quiet morning. By 9.30 a.m. there were over 2000 of the poor and oppressed gathered at Porta della Finestra. They would listen to some speeches and then enjoy themselves, eating and drinking the day away. At 10 a.m., the leader of the Popular Front took the stand to make the first speech. Fifteen minutes later, as he opened his mouth, a seventy-year-old woman in the crowd fell over, shot dead. Behind her lay a thirteen-year-old girl, half her face blown away. Old men tumbled over, their intestines spilling out. Concealed in the rocks above the crowd, Giuliano's men were carrying out a massacre. Ten minutes later, it was all over. There were eleven killed outright and fifty-five others wounded, some of whom died later.

Shortly afterwards, three young men and a local prostitute who were on their way up to the meeting saw a strange sight: twelve armed men in American uniforms, and one in a white raincoat, came scrambling down the mountainside. The onlookers concealed themselves. They had just seen Giuliano and his band returning from their bloody work. His actions were wholly successful: the Popular Front had a disastrous election.

For the next two years, Giuliano was a popular man among the landlords, the Mafia, and (however distasteful it was) the occupying American forces; there would be no Communism in Sicily. But Giuliano finally outlived his usefulness, and became an embarrassment to his former allies. The police could not catch him, or find witnesses to testify against him. But they finally managed to buy the treasonable services of his lieutenant, Pisciotta. For fifty million lire he agreed to kill the bandit king. At 3.19 on the morning of 5 July 1950, Pisciotta shot Giuliano twice in the chest as he lay sleeping in a safe house in the town of Castelvetrano. The police then hastily hauled the dead bandit out of bed, dressed him, took him outside and sprayed him with machine-gun fire to try and conceal Pisciotta's treachery, so that he might live to enjoy his reward. Unfortunately, the corpse refused to bleed dramatically enough, and they were obliged to slit the throat of a chicken and pour its contents all over Giuliano.

Don Calò was relieved to see the bandit die. Latterly, his power had been so great that when he was disowned by his Christian Democrat supporters, Giuliano had openly threatened to abduct and kill its backers, including Don Calò. The latter, having helped create this monster, was reduced to hiding from him and travelled concealed in the backs of vegetable lorries. A year after the bandit died, Don Calò also went to the grave, though somewhat more peacefully.

Inclined to over-indulge and take little exercise, he had grown sluggish and corpulent. While travelling to Villalba one day, he asked that his car be stopped so that he could assume a comfortable supine position on the verge. Lying there, his vast belly pointing skywards, he sighed deeply, murmured "How beautiful life is!" and promptly expired. His funeral was a state occasion attended by all of significance, and his plaque in the church at Villalba declares, without irony, his many virtues; he was chaste, temperate, forbearing, tireless in his defence of the weak and, above all, a gentleman.

Chapter Two

FROM "LUCKY" TO GOTTI: A MISCELLANY OF AMERICAN MAFIOSI

The American Mafia, the most powerful criminal organization in the world, owes its present strength to the pioneering efforts of Charles "Lucky" Luciano, who in the first half of this century transformed a collection of feuding extortionists and racketeers into a multi-billion dollar corporation.

He was born Salvatore Lucania in East Harlem, New York, into a large and poor family; his father was a construction worker and his mother supplemented their meagre income by taking in laundry. At the age of fifteen, he was thrown out of the house by his father who despaired at his son's drift into crime; not even the severest of beatings seemed to inhibit him. His mother continued to adore him, and smuggled jars of her home-made pasta sauce (the one thing he missed) to her errant son.

He rented his own apartment and formed his own *borgata*: a gang of young, street-wise criminals. Many of the New York Mafia's foremost members began their careers in Luciano's borgata: Frank Costello, Gaetano "Three Fingers Brown" Lucchese, Albert Anastasia and Vito Genovese.

For fear of shaming his family name, the embryonic mobster changed his surname from Lucania to Luciano. He

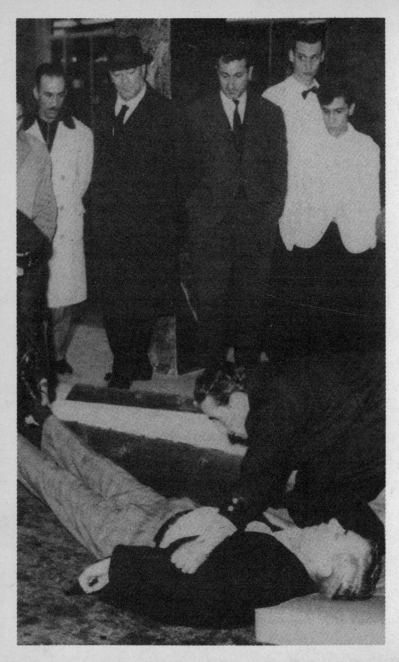

The end of a gangster – Charles 'Lucky' Luciano

From its earliest days in America, much of the Mafia's wealth was founded upon illegal gambling rackets, the most basic of which was the "numbers" game that predominated in the black ghettos. Tickets, costing between twenty-five cents and a dollar, were sold at barber shops and candy stores. It was a simple variety of lottery: the participant would select up to three digits from one to ten, with odds thus ranging from ten to one to a thousand to one. The winning number was determined by the last three digits of an established daily number that could not in theory be fixed, such as the circulation of a newspaper or the day's sale of US Treasury stocks. The profit was the difference between tickets sold and winnings paid out. With no tax and low overheads the income could be vast.

also decided he hated being called Salvatore, as it was too often shorted to "Sal", and re-christened himself Charles; he later acquired his nickname "Lucky" by surviving an assassination attempt by knife. Lucky stood head and shoulders above his confederates; he possessed extraordinary business acumen and a capacity for organization. By the age of eighteen he was a czar of petty crime and was formulating plans for a nation-wide confederacy of hoodlums. He even made the unprecedented move of forming an alliance with two Jewish mobsters, Meyer Lansky and Benjamin "Bugsy" Siegel, from the Lower East Side.

Within a few years, Lucky went to work for the don of the "amici", the boss of the Mafia, Giuseppe "Joe the Boss"

Salvatore "Sally" De Vita was a most unusual
hood. An incredibly ugly man, he was the only
known Mafia transvestite, and spent much of his
time off duty trying to disguise himself as a
woman. He wore blonde wigs, rouge, mascara,
lipstick and a padded bra, and owned wardrobes
full of stunning designer dresses, mostly stolen.
But it was unwise to tease him excessively: he
invariably carried a loaded pistol in his Gucci
handbag.

Masseria, who insisted on patronizing Lucky by calling him
bambino. Masseria, who was rampantly anti-semitic, hated
Siegel and Lansky and insisted that Lucky "get rid of those
fucking hebes". Lucky detested Masseria and had the
pleasure of arranging for him to be murdered on the
orders of Salvatore Maranzano, who succeeded him to
the throne of power. Masseria was shot in a restaurant
where he thought he was joining Lucky for a plate of pasta.
Lucky got up mid-way through the meal and went to the
toilet; while he was in there the restaurant was raked with
gunfire.

Maranzano, an elegant figure, was something of a Sicilian
traditionalist, and Lucky, while having nothing personal
against him, could see that there was little prospect of the
man instigating any of the modern business plans that
Lucky had his heart set on. Maranzano read Roman history
for inspiration, whilst Lucky dreamed of a modern empire of
crime, sheltered by accountants and lawyers. Lucky had to
take the throne by force: in September 1931 Maranzano and
his supporters died, on an occasion that was thereafter
remembered as "The Night of the Sicilian Vespers". Four
men, disguised as members of the Internal Revenue, visited

Maranzano and knifed him to death; some forty of his associates were also murdered. At the age of thirty-four, Lucky Luciano was the head of the New York Mafia, which he eventually welded into the most powerful criminal organization ever known.

He was finally brought down by the efforts of a determined District Attorney, Thomas E. Dewy, who nailed him on charges of running a prostitution ring; but Lucky's luxurious sojourn in New York's Clinton State prison set the tone for incarcerated mafiosi. He had a private cell with an electric stove, curtains over the cell door and a pet canary. Dressed in a tailor-made prison uniform of silk shirt and highly polished shoes, he was guarded round the clock by paid bodyguards, and held formal audiences in the prison exercise yard, bestowing favours like a monarch.

Perhaps his greatest achievement – for it enabled the uninterrupted pursuit of illicit wealth – was the peace he forged between the Mafia clans. But as the network of organized crime expanded, his position – that of *capo di tutti i capi* (the boss of all bosses) – became an increasingly attractive post.

When he was sent to prison, the Second World War had started, and the Mafia was approached by the US Government for assistance at home and abroad. They wanted the cooperation of the Sicilian Mafia in the event of Allied landings and they also wanted the Mafia to provide the eyes and ears for a counter-intelligence operation along the New York waterfront, to balk anticipated acts of sabotage by German and Italian agents. The Mafia agreed; its secret pay-off was to be the release of Lucky Luciano, to which the Government acquiesced on condition that he was returned to Italy.

On 9 February 1946, Luciano was transported from his upstate New York prison cell to Brooklyn where he was to be put on an ocean-liner with a one-way ticket to Italy. The

Carlo Gambino, the figure said to have inspired Brando's portrayal of Don Corleone in *The Godfather*, arrived in America as a twenty-two-year-old stowaway in 1924. He was a loyal Mafia member from the start, a waterfront hood, a leading capo and finally a brilliant strategist who took control of the entire Mafia. His business intelligence was second to none. During Prohibition he managed to corner the market in distilled alcohol, buying at fifteen dollars per tin and selling at fifty. During the Second World War he set up a huge black market racket using forged ration stamps, netting himself millions of dollars. He took the Mafia further into the twilight world of quasi-legality, where the profit from illegal activities could be laundered and invested legally to create yet more money. Under him, the Mafia consolidated its grip on the unions, some of whom were happy to let their pension funds be invested at his discretion. A modest, soft-spoken man, Gambino was the subject of police investigations for forty years, but his last stint in prison was in 1937. They never pinned anything on him after that: it was impossible to find anyone insane enough to testify against this endearing, kind old gentleman. When police came to question him at his unassuming Brooklyn house they could always count on being received courteously and offered some of Mrs Gambino's excellent homemade cookies. But while he detested flashiness and unnecessary violence in business, as a Mafia disciplinarian Gambino was utterly

> ruthless, and countless numbers died on his
> whispered orders. One man who attempted to
> seduce wives of imprisoned mafiosi was
> subjected, on Gambino's orders, to the most
> horrible death, being slowly fed while alive into
> a large meat grinder, feet first.

entire high command of the New York Mafia turned out to
see Lucky off: Albert Anastasia, Vito Genovese, Joseph
Profaci, Joseph Bonanno, Frank Costello and Joe Adonis.
Also present were two fast-rising mobsters, Carlo Gambino
and Thomas Lucchese.

Lucky stayed put in Rome for a while, but then began to
creep back towards the US and turned up in Cuba, run by
the corrupt Batista, where the Mafia had invested heavily in
casinos and hotels. But he was too close for the comfort of
the US authorities, and they encouraged the Cubans to
return him to Italy. In January 1962, Lucky Luciano went to
the Naples airport to await the arrival of an American film
producer interested in making a film based on the gangster's
life. To general consternation, he dropped dead of a heart
attack in the airport lounge.

Lucky had been concerned that in his absence the Mafia
would begin to tear itself apart. No sooner was his ship out
of the harbour than his worst fears came true. The arrogant
Vito Genovese was not only making a pitch for the position
of "capo di tutti i capi", but was also demanding that the
Mafia move into the rapidly expanding narcotics market,
and wanted to see the fruitful partnership that Lucky had
formed with the Jewish mobsters broken. His demands
found little favour with Frank Costello, the Mafia don of
Manhattan, who had been one of those closest to Lucky and
who commanded great influence and respect, both inside
and outside the Mafia. Costello was known as the "prime

minister of the underworld" for his skill in defusing potentially explosive disputes. He was an affable and cautious man who detested violence, and had assiduously courted police and politicians so that New York's authorities turned a blind eye to Mafia activities, so long as they stayed clear of drugs and kept the violence internal and to a minimum. Moreover, he liked the Jews and appreciated their business acumen. The Mafia had learned much from them, particularly the importance of maintaining a quasi-legality in its activities, infiltrating legitimate businesses wherever possible.

Costello made an enemy in Genovese, who in turn found an ally in Anastasia. Their resentment — and ambition — festered, and in 1957 they decided to make a play for power. On 2 May Costello was attacked in the lobby of his hotel by a notoriously stupid hood, an ex-boxer called Vincent "the Chin" Gigante. He shot Costello at point-blank range in the head. He hit him squarely in the temple, but, miraculously, the bullet pierced only the skin, made a complete circuit of the head under the surface, and finally re-emerged at its entry point. The Chin was unaware of this: he left Costello for dead. Costello told the police that he had no idea who would want to kill a dull businessman such as himself, and immediately made plans to retire. He had got the message, and died peacefully twenty years later.

Anastasia was a wholly deranged individual and the failure of the attempt on Costello sent him off the deep end. He became paranoid that he would be killed in retribution, and took steps to eliminate anyone he thought posed a physical threat to him. It was a bloodbath. As his violence and demands for power increased, it was decided that something must be done. Finally one of his capi, Carlo Gambino, arranged for the elimination of Albert Anastasia, nominally on the grounds that he had been charging a $40,000 fee for entry into his Mafia

family — an unforgivable lapse in traditional protocol.
Gambino turned to the most infamous killers around, the
Gallo brothers: "Crazy Joe", "Kid Twist" and "Kid Blast".
In October 1957 they walked into a barber's in a
Manhattan hotel, where Anastasia was having his morn-
ing shave, and, while a towel was over his head, blew his
brains out.

Gambino died peacefully in 1976, and his son-in-law Paul
Castellano, also from the Gambino family, became "capo di
tutti i capi". Castellano was a man very much in the mould
of Carlo Gambino. He was diplomatic by instinct and liked a
quiet life, unlike Gambino's long-time lieutenant, Aniello
Dellacroce, the mentor of John Gotti, future head of the
Gambino clan and Mafia don in the making.

Aniello Dellacroce (which literally means, in Sicilian
Italian, "little lamb of the cross") was Gambino's number
two for many years. His unadulterated sadism provided
an admirable foil for the smooth charms of the don. Born
in Italy, Dellacroce drifted into crime while still a boy
and by his late teens was a Mafia hood specializing in
strong-arm work and killing, for which he had a considerable gift, and which he obviously enjoyed. He
would fix his bulging eyes on his victim and, in carefully
modulated tones, would tell the man exactly how he was
going to die; first he would shoot him in the knees, then
in the stomach, and, after pausing to savour the pain he
had inflicted, he would occasionally consent to adminis-
tering a *coup de grâce* in the head. When an enforcer for
the vicious hood Alberto Anastasia, Dellacroce had been
delegated to "manage" his casinos. He would punish
bent dealers and croupiers by smashing their hands with
a sledgehammer.

Once, upon finding the corpse of one of his victims,
police were convinced it had been decapitated. Pathol-
ogists later found the remains of the head beaten into
the chest cavity. Another corpse could only be identified

John Gotti goes on trial on charges of orchestrating the slaying of Castellano as well as other racketeering charges

by teeth found inside its stomach. Curiously, when travelling incognito, Dellacroce liked to dress up as a catholic priest.

Dellacroce – and, under him, Gotti – made millions for the Mafia from dealing in heroin. Publicly, the Mafia has always forbidden its members to deal in drugs, upon penalty of death. It has given the impression that gambling, protection rackets and large-scale swindles were the foundation of its wealth, and that its activities have become increasingly legal. One reason to discourage its members from dealing in narcotics is the long sentence the crime carries. Faced with forty years in prison, a criminal can be tempted to turn informer in exchange for immunity.

But in reality, the Mafia has from its first days in America been involved with narcotics. There is too much money to be made, too easily: a kilo of the opium base for heroin costs $12,000 at its source in the Middle East or Southeast Asia. After being processed and cut with other substances until it is only three and a half per cent heroin, the same kilo will fetch two million dollars on the streets.

Mafia bosses generally stayed carefully in the background, and avoided being seen to be involved in the trade. Instead, the Mafia would normally operate in association with some other branch of organized crime. Since the mid-1950s, the Mafia has controlled the American heroin trade at a discreet distance. It reorganized the supply line, linking up with the powerful Corsican heroin dealers, and established processing laboratories in Sicily staffed with French drug chemists. The "French Connection" was created and the Mafia flooded the streets of urban America with high-quality "smack". The number of heroin addicts in the United States rose from fifty thousand in the 1950s to something near half a million.

The son of poor immigrants from Southern Italy, John Gotti was born in New York in 1940. Brought up in East Harlem and Brooklyn, he quickly became known for his

In 1980 Gotti's already unstable temperament was heightened by personal tragedy: his twelve-year-old son Frank was accidentally run over by one of his neighbours, a man called John Favara. Favara was utterly distraught, but his expressions of remorse and sympathy met with angry silence. Later, his car was stolen, and "murderer" scrawled across it. He found a black-edged picture of the dead boy in his mail-box. Rumours began circulating that he was about to be killed. He decided to move, but on the very day that he sold his house, three men in a van rolled up to his work-place. He pulled a gun, but his shots went wild. Bludgeoned insensible, he was thrown into the back of the van and never seen again.

volcanic temper. He seemed to be in a constant rage, and was uncontrollable at school, though he was by no means unintelligent and had an IQ of around 140. A born leader, he soon attracted a group of equally wild companions and formed a "borgata".

After his father, John Gotti, moved his family to the violent waterfront district of Brooklyn and then the even meaner streets of East New York, Gotti joined a tough gang, the "Fulton Rockaway Boys". They ran minor extortion rackets, stole and hijacked, organized a little illegal gambling (taking care in all of these not to intrude on Mafia territory), and, above all, fought territorial battles with other gangs for the right to parade up and down their grim home turf.

Gotti was soon leader of the "borgata". Quite apart from his canniness and naked aggression he stood out for his appalling taste in clothing: he wore anything, so long as it was loud, colourful and stolen. Purple suits were a favourite. He attracted the attention of Carmine "Charley Wagons" Fatico, an associate of the late Alberto Anastasia. Although only seventeen, Gotti quickly proved his worth as a strong man, performing one or two spectacular beatings, and became one of the 120 men Fatico had working for him. Fatico had a well-established organization, which grossed him around thirty million dollars annually. The money came from hijacking, illegal gambling and loan-sharking, but Fatico had a special line in gay bars. Homosexuality was still illegal in America, and Fatico's discreet string of private gay clubs, where exotic stage acts could be seen by men prepared to pay exotic prices for admission and drinks, was highly lucrative. Ironically, it would be at one of his bars, the Stonewall Inn, that gay men in 1969 began the gay rights movement.

Throughout his early years Gotti was in and out of prison, principally on charges of theft and hijacking. His time in jail gave him the opportunity to meet a whole host of mafiosi, who, in turn, remembered the explosive and capable young man. When Carmine Fatico began to ail, Gotti was put in charge of the outfit, and along with a number of other middle-ranking hoods he successfully organized a lucrative narcotics channel into New York. He went to great lengths to ensure that Castellano was not aware of the narcotics trade; he even publicly banished one of his crew on the grounds that he was a drugs dealer. By 1979 Gotti, although little more than a Mafia soldier, was already rumoured to be Dellacroce's chosen successor as underboss of the Gambino clan, a remarkable rate of progress since he had only been "made" (formally initiated into the Mafia) two years beforehand.

Gotti's principal weakness was gambling. He could blow $30,000 a day on betting and at one point in the 1982

American football season Gotti had lost a quarter of a million dollars. He and his brother ran an illegal casino in Little Italy. Gotti could not resist betting against his own house and on one night lost $55,000.

Dellacroce died of cancer in 1985. At the same time, Gotti's narcotics network had been uncovered by the police and he and several other Mafia members were facing trial. Castellano, furious at the heroin-trafficking, had come to regard Gotti as a substantial embarrassment. It was only a matter of time before he had him killed. With his protector Dellacroce gone, Gotti felt exposed and decided to strike first. He rapidly established the necessary support for his actions throughout the Mafia membership, alternately seducing and threatening, and convinced many that the ageing Castellano was too afflicted by conscience and needed replacing.

On 16 December 1985, Castellano arrived outside Sparks Restaurant in New York. Getting out of his chauffeur-driven car, he encountered three men in identical overcoats and fur hats. They fired six shots into his body. He died instantly. The men then shot his chauffeur dead and melted away. Gotti did not attend his funeral.

By Christmas 1985, John Gotti was head of the most powerful criminal organization in the world. In April 1992, he was convicted of murder and racketeering, and sentenced to life without parole. His case is currently under appeal.

Castellano's funeral was a modest affair, unlike most Mafia funerals. The standard for these events was set in 1928 by the spectacular last rites of Brooklyn mobster Frank Uale, who was shot to death. There were two hundred cars in his funeral procession, thirty-eight of which carried the flowers, and several thousand mourners. He was buried in a casket of silver and nickel, costing $15,000; the whole occasion cost $200,000.

Chapter Three

MURDER
INCORPORATED

J ust before the First World War, the overcrowded
population of the predominantly Jewish quarter of the
Lower East Side in New York's Manhattan and the
Italian neighbourhoods of Little Italy and East Harlem
began to overflow and move eastwards, across the East
River and into the vast interior plains of Brooklyn. Here for
generations the quiet villages of Williamsburg, Brownsville
and East New York had existed in a rural torpor which was
soon dispelled. With the immigrants came organized crime,
and by 1930 the Italian Mafia and the Jewish mobs were
flourishing alongside one another. Though they had often
fought, they were, for the most part, content to come to
mutually beneficial arrangements in the pursuit of profit.

The Italian Mafia concentrated on its conventional
interests, primarily loan-sharking and illegal gambling,
while the Jewish mobsters derived their wealth from
extortion, principally targeting the small garment manufacturers. Many of these had fled over the river in order to
escape from the Garment Center in Manhattan, which had
for years been under the control of mobsters like Louis
"Lepke" Buchalter, who was used by the manufacturers to
break strikes, and then found that he could make money by
charging the manufacturers for his protection.

The manufacturers who fled across the river did not
elude Buchalter for long. He came after them, but in
Brooklyn he found that seven local punks were already
attempting to run a protection racket involving clothing

By the mid-1930s, Louis Buchalter was extorting nearly fifty million dollars a year from the New York garment manufacturers in return for guaranteeing that there would be no disruption of labour. He had nearly 250 vicious hoods in his employment, including the infamous Jacob Shapiro, his chief lieutenant, who walked around with lead window-sash weights in his pockets which he used to smash in the skulls of manufacturers and union leaders unwilling to cooperate.

manufacturers. Buchalter was deeply offended at this intrusion into his private territory, and accordingly made plans to have them eliminated. But the killing of the seven posed problems. While he was blessed with strong-arm men who could be relied on to break heads effectively, Buchalter was short of talented, discreet killers who could perform their task efficiently, without upsetting the authorities and leaving a trail of bloody footprints that would lead the police to his door.

To solve this problem, Buchalter opened negotiations with the Mafia, represented by its rising star in Brooklyn, Albert Anastasia, a capo from the waterfront rackets. Buchalter proposed that the Italians and the Jews should pool their talents and create a combined force of Italian and Jewish professional killers, who would work — for a price — for both individuals and organized crime syndicates. Anastasia accepted, and Murder Incorporated was born.

The organization fused murder with corporate methods. Buchalter was president and Anastasia chief executive officer, and they had a staff of selected, smart killers, who were put on annual $12,000 retainers. There were

Each assignment was called a "contract", a euphemism which rapidly passed into common usage, along with "hit", the Murder Incorporated official parlance for the actual killing. The killers retained by Murder Incorporated were the cream of New York's hit-men. Among them were Vito "Chicken Head" Gurino, who earned his nickname because he perfected his aim by blasting the heads off live chickens, and Frank "The Dasher" Abbanando, so called because once, when his gun misfired during a hit and the victim pursued him around a building, Abbanando was faster, and succeeded in lapping him; he came up behind his pursuer and shot him in the back of the head.

strict corporate rules: murder was only to be committed for "business reasons", and "civilians" were not to be harmed in the course of the hit.

The policy on each job submitted was jointly agreed by president and chief executive, who rationally and coldly considered the ramifications of requests for killing within the sphere of organized crime. If they accepted the job, the execution was assigned to a team of assassins.

The organization's star killer was Abraham "Kid Twist" Reles. Fat, five foot two inches tall, with thick lips, a flat, broken nose and gangling arms, Reles derived his nickname from his habit of munching boxfuls of chocolate candy twists. He specialized in the use of the ice-pick, which he jammed into his victim's heart. Reles showed no mercy, and when people saw him walking down the street they were inclined to cross to the opposite pavement. Everybody

Anastasia (left) walks out of the federal Court on 23rd May 1955

Albert Anastasia, the Mafia's "King of Brooklyn", was also known as "The Mad Hatter" or "The Executioner". A homicidal maniac with a violent temper, he liked killing for the sake of killing and ordered deaths on the slightest pretext. After reading in the newspaper that a local citizen had recognized the famous bank robber Willie Smith and turned him in to the police, Anastasia ordered that this conscientious citizen be immediately killed. "I hate a rat," he said, "no matter who he is." He liked to have murder victims hideously tortured before their death and when unable to participate himself he insisted that every detail of the torture be later recounted to him; he particularly relished it when they begged for mercy. He lived like an emperor near New York Harbour in New Jersey, in a vast house surrounded by a seven-foot barbed-wire fence, a pack of Dobermans and a permanent bodyguard. His money came from the waterfront rackets: extortion, theft, gambling, loan-sharking and kick-backs. The 40,000 longshoremen who worked in the port were all under his thumb. Also, his brother "Tough Tony" was president of the biggest union and he was thought to have the entire roll-call of local police and politicians on his payroll.

knew that Reles had once openly killed two black men without any provocation: one of them had worked at a car wash and failed to spot a small smudge on the front fender of Reles' car, the other had worked at a parking lot and had failed to move fast enough when Reles ordered him to fetch his Cadillac.

It will never be known how many people Murder Incorporated killed during the peak years of business, between 1935 and 1939. Some estimates are as high as 300, but only about a dozen or so murders – including that of Arthur "Dutch Schultz" Fleigenheimer – have actually been laid at its door. Its "employees" swaggered around the streets of Brooklyn, untroubled by the police, who generally avoided them. There were nearly 200 "employees", because, apart from the elite killers, there were "fingermen" who charted the movements of prospective victims, "wheelmen" who stole the cars used in the hits and "evaporators" who tidied up after the crime and ensured that the body of the victim disappeared.

Murder Incorporated might still be terrorizing America, were it not for the arrest of the erratic Abe Reles. The lethal Kid Twist was forever committing non-sanctioned murders, casual killings over and above his Murder Incorporated quota. The police picked him up for one of these; the evidence was indisputable, and Reles faced the electric chair. In return for immunity from prosecution, Kid Twist agreed to turn stool-pigeon and tell everything he knew about Murder Incorporated. His sensational revelations allowed the police to crush the organization, and Louis Buchalter went to the electric chair.

But Reles never lived to enjoy the new life the authorities had promised him. After spilling the beans on Murder Incorporated, he began to blab about the Mafia, and mentioned specific people, including Albert Anastasia, to the Brooklyn District Attorney, William O'Dwyer. Too late he learned that O'Dwyer had allegedly gone straight out and sold the glad news of Reles' revelations to Anastasia. The Mafia boss paid the corrupt attorney $100,000 for the silencing of Kid Twist.

On 11 November 1941, Kid Twist mysteriously fell from the seventh-floor window of a Coney Island hotel, where he was being concealed by the District Attorney's office under a twenty-four hour guard. Although the murder case remains officially unsolved to this day, it was alleged that O'Dwyer or Anastasia arranged for two or three corrupt police officers to defenestrate the stool-pigeon before he said any more.

The death ended any further investigation into Murder Incorporated, but Reles remained a legendary figure in New York. Throughout Brooklyn, gangsters would raise their glasses and say: "Here's to Abe Reles, a great canary. He could sing, but he couldn't fly."

Chapter Four

"BUGSY" SIEGEL: CASANOVA MOBSTER

B enjamin "Bugsy" Siegel (he hated being called Bugsy, a name he acquired in his early mob days) was the most suave and charming of criminals. Intelligent, cosmopolitan, Jewish and handsome, he effortlessly infiltrated American society. The titled loved him, and he enjoyed the trust of the most hard-bitten and cynical of businessmen. To movie stars he was tangible proof of the reality of the romantic hoods they played. Many, such as Cary Grant, were close friends though sometimes they became frightened as to where their friendship with this man might take them. Siegel once told Del Webb that he had personally killed twelve men. When Webb's face betrayed his fear, Siegel looked at him and laughed.

"There's no chance that you'll get killed," he told him. "We only kill each other."

Benjamin Siegel was born on 28 February 1906 in the Jewish Williamsburg district of Brooklyn, then a labyrinth of crowded tenements, street pedlars, delicatessens and synagogues. He left home without finishing school, and joined a band of other juvenile delinquents who prowled the East Side in Manhattan at night. His first crime was a stick-up in a loan company office, and he was soon "rolling" drunks, committing burglaries and vigorously participating in the perpetual, violent gang wars.

On one foray he met another young hood, George Ranft, who later changed his name to Raft and became the

Hollywood star. Siegel and Raft became the closest of
buddies. Many years later, when Raft was a national
celebrity, his aging mother saw him being escorted into
a cinema by an honorary guard of four policemen. So
accustomed was she to thinking of her son as a criminal that
her first reaction was to shout "Run, Georgie, run!"

From Siegel's earliest days he became known for his
love of horse-play and his sheer effrontery towards the
police. Later, when a major player in crime, he would still
amuse himself by leaning out of the windows of hotels
and dropping water-bombs on the heads of the snooping
police.

By rights, Siegel should have remained a petty crook and
tearaway, just one of the other thousands of struggling
street bums from the Jewish and Italian ghettos. But during
the days of Prohibition – there was never a single edict
more favourable to organized crime – he made the transi-
tion from punk to swaggering gangster.

During this era the Lower East Side was dominated by
two ruthless mobs: the Italians – the Mafia – led by Lucky
Luciano, Vito Genovese and Albert Anastasia, and the
Jewish mob, headed by Louis Buchalter and Jacob Shapiro, known as the "Gold Dust Twins". It was as part of this
group that Siegel encountered Meyer Lansky, his long-time
associate. Together they split away and formed the "Bug-
Meyer Mob".

Little hard evidence of the extent of his early criminal
activities survives, though his mob had a fearful reputation.
He was regularly picked up by the police for such offences
as possessing concealed weapons, and at the age of nineteen was accused of rape by a local girl. When the case came
to court, the witnesses had mysteriously vanished. The only
conviction he ever suffered was for illegal gambling, when
he was picked up by the police during a raid on a Miami
hotel. Even then he gave a false name and was fined only
$100.

Furthermore, as Siegel ascended the hierarchy of crime, his file at New York Police Department, which should have bulged with the records of his arrests and various suspected offences, grew perversely thinner. Over the years, this smartest of gangsters managed to wipe his past record clean, arranging, by legal and illegal means, to have past offences deleted, pictures withheld and charge sheets appropriated. The only official memento of his early career now remaining to the New York Police is a solitary mugshot.

Still in his twenties, Siegel already had a suite at the Waldorf-Astoria, two floors below his mentor, Lucky Luciano. He wore coats with velvet collars, handmade shirts and sharp, pointed and highly glossed shoes. He had a special line in hats and favoured a snap-brim, a style he had picked up from the Broadway columnist, Mark Hellinger, one of the first of many friends in show-business. Broadway was a great melting-pot for the legal and illegal sectors of society. Criminals, celebrities, politicians, magnates, actors and actresses – anyone who was news – mingled and networked at the same parties and the same restaurants and clubs. They dressed alike, and thought alike. They were drawn by the same things: the craving for success, recognition and the good life that money could buy. More than one major movie cr Broadway show was financed by the proceeds from speakeasies, extortion and murder.

The Siegel-Meyer mob hauled liquor and supplied armed convoys for other groups trucking it between New York and Philadelphia. The gang also had a wholesale liquor business of their own and operated a string of illicit stills and a smuggling network. They were in business for money, and though they happily committed robberies, hijackings and murders these were less for profit than to assert their identity and discourage any major competitors in the truly lucrative field of bootlegging. Siegel's earnings

One of the boldest robberies of the 1930s took place on the morning of 24 August 1934 in Brooklyn, New York. Just after noon, an armoured car from the United States Trucking Company arrived to collect cash from the Rubel Ice Company on Bay and Nineteenth Street. Before leaving the vehicle the guards scanned the area; everything looked normal, and one guard entered the building while the other waited outside. At this moment, a kerbside pedlar threw a sack off his cart revealing two machine guns. Other men who had looked like innocent loiterers ran up with drawn guns. In a few minutes, bags of money were transferred from the armoured car to two cars belonging to the robbers. By the time the guard emerged from the Ice Company, the cars were speeding away. The New York police were on the scene within minutes, looking for the two cars, but the gang was already unloading the money at a pier less than a mile away into two waiting boats. The gang took their haul to a New Jersey hideout, and found that they had netted just under half a million dollars. The robbers then split up, taking an oath not to speak of their part in the hold-up.

Two years later, the police began to learn the names of men they believed had taken part in the robbery: John Manning, a top criminal, Joseph Kress, who had stolen the cars, two ex-bootleggers called John Hughes and Thomas Quinn, John and Francis Oley, kidnapper Percy Geary and forger Stewart Wallace. Most of these

> men were later imprisoned for other crimes,
> but remained loyal to their oath of denying all
> knowledge of the crime. John Manning, who was
> almost certainly the planner, was shot and killed
> in a gang feud on 6 July 1936.

were near the one million dollar mark. He once told a friend that, had he not taken a beating in the Wall Street crash, he would have happily gone "legit".

Like any high profile gangster he had his enemies and his life was always at risk, and in these early years Siegel was constantly on the move, shifting between his apartment on Eighty-fifth Street, the Waldorf, his headquarters near Lewis Street on the Lower East Side, and the various hideouts and offices of his criminal associates. He kept his family – his wife Esta and his two daughters – tucked out of sight in an expensive house in Scarsdale. In the early 1930s, Bugsy survived a number of attempts on his life: his car was shot up by machine-gun fire, and a bomb was placed in a room in which he was hosting a meeting of senior mobsters (he escaped with minor injuries, and apparently was able to slip unseen out of the hospital to avenge himself on the would-be assassin, before returning to his sick bed – a perfect alibi).

Siegel, like many Jewish mobsters, preferred to settle disagreements by negotiation, but would not hesitate to order the execution of problematic individuals. In 1934 Joey and Louis "Pretty" Amberg, minor drug pedlars and extortionists from Brownsville, who had already demanded a cut of a fee charged by Siegel's gang for a piece of strong arm strike-breaking in their territory, exasperated his patience when they killed one of his henchmen. Joey was called into Bugsy's office, forced to confess and then summarily shot; Louis was finely diced with an axe.

Gangsters

When Prohibition came to an end, the Mafia and their associates – and Siegel was still an ally – needed to replace their lost income. They began to look more closely at the previously minor areas of narcotics, prostitution, casinos, union enforcement and even wholesale murder for the right money (Murder Incorporated was one result). They also looked to expand westwards, into California.

In 1936 Bugsy Siegel moved to California. California seemed a territory ripe for crime and Bugsy didn't want to stay in New York and end up dead on the streets, nor did he enjoy the company of fellow gangsters. He always thought a little more of himself, and craved respectability. For Siegel, Hollywood was a natural home: here people could re-invent their pasts freely, and a little urbanity, good looks and a lot of money bought acceptance. Furthermore, he had a weakness for actresses, and had recently formed an association with Ketti Gallian, a French starlet. He was to spend $50,000 vainly trying to launch her career in movies.

Siegel settled down in Beverly Hills, living in a house rented from the famous singer, Lawrence Tibbet. He styled himself a "sportsman" and bon viveur, and joined the exclusive Hillcrest Country Club. His daughters attended the best private school and he socialized with George Raft, Jean Harlow and Clark Gable. Jean Harlow had a particular affection for Bugsy and was thought to have been the godmother of his daughter Millicent. Siegel also made the acquaintance of the millionairess and socialite Countess Dorothy Dendice Taylor DiFrasso. Tired of her marriage, and jaded with her fortune, this buxom and frosty eyed woman frequently visited her mansion in Beverly Hills, where she organized elaborate entertainment – such as bare fist boxing – for her celebrity guests. She had an unhappy affair with Gary Cooper, and was casting around for something a little out of the ordinary, when she was introduced to Siegel. Within days, the semi-literate gangster

Benjamin ''Bugsy'' Siegel

Gangsters

The Countess DiFrasso was in love with Siegel and in 1938 bankrolled one of his more extravagant schemes: the search for a legendary ninety-million-dollar treasure supposedly buried on an island off Costa Rica. Equipped with a treasure map supplied by an old soak called Bill Bowbeer, the couple assembled an extraordinary entourage of fellow speculators, chartered a boat and set off for Cocos Island, where, Siegel told the company, concealed in a cave was this fabulous treasure. After several weeks of sailing, the motley crew of socialites and crooks reached the deserted, inhospitable island. Its shore was rocky, and the land was covered by thick jungle and creepers. They spent ten horrible days looking for the gold; few on board had actually expected to find anything, but it quickly became apparent that Siegel had been in deadly earnest. His temper rose rapidly as the fruitless search continued. They dug everywhere in temperatures approaching ninety degrees, eaten alive by mosquitoes and plagued by tropical sickness. The Countess retreated to the boat and sat in the shade, drinking champagne and wilting. Finally, having dynamited large portions of the island, the furious Siegel was forced to abandon the search. The expedition cost the Duchess at least $50,000.

from New York, driven by an enormous need for social acceptance, was in her bed. He was literally sleeping his way to the top.

"Bugsy" Siegel: Casanova Mobster

Siegel still had "business" interests in New York, mainly protection rackets, from which he derived a steady income. But with his taste for the glamorous life, the cost of the mansion he was building, the education of his family and the endless string of girlfriends to be discreetly maintained, he always needed more. He was also a compulsive gambler who could spend $2,000–$5,000 a day on football and horses. But for the moment, he was on a winning streak.

He had interests in pieces of property in California, which brought in a little, but his first major coup was to invest heavily — with money borrowed from unfortunate friends like George Raft — in a series of off-shore, floating casinos: gambling ships, which stood outside the state's jurisdiction. He made a small fortune, but Raft, who was always in money troubles and had been virtually forced to invest in the ship, never saw a cent of profit. Indeed he was lucky to get his original stake back: his $20,000 was returned to him in tiny instalments over a period of months. Bugsy might have been extravagant, but he was never unduly generous.

Siegel, the most assiduous social climber of his day, kept lists of people he wished to meet — and bed — and even managed to inveigle his way into the house of Jack Warner, the movie mogul, quite against Warner's wishes. Siegel managed to conceal his criminal association from his new Californian neighbours, but a reporter on the *Los Angeles Examiner* received a tip-off from a mysterious informant and a front-page exposé followed; Bugsy found that his local reputation was taking a dip. He decided to spend some time away and, leaving his family behind, he took off with the Countess DiFrasso to Italy and thence all over Europe. Initially, the reason for the trip was to try and sell the patent of a new explosive, "Atomite", which he had interested the Countess in, to Mussolini. The Countess, feeling that she should be seen to be travelling with someone of her own class, bestowed a bogus baronetcy on Bugsy, who enjoyed going under the title Bart Siegel, English aristocrat. The

Bugsy Siegel was supremely vain. A fanatic on the subject of physical fitness and virility, he smoked and drank little, worked-out in the boxing ring and spent every afternoon in the gym, where he held many of his business meetings. At night-time he rubbed beauty cream into his face and put on an elastic chin strap to keep his features from sagging. Unless he was out on the town he went to bed at 10 p.m., having spent an hour or so struggling with a self-improvement book (he was continually trying to extend his vocabulary and lose the New York accent that betrayed his origins). He had a horror of going bald, and nobody was allowed to mention his receding hairline. Anyone with a full head of hair would be aware of his jealous gaze and he once paid an associate who had a full complement of hair $2500 to allow him to cut a mass of it off.

explosive was another expensive disaster for the Countess, and they had to cut short their stay in Rome because Siegel, seeing that Goering and Goebbels were also paying a visit, decided that one or both of them needed killing. Whatever his crimes, Siegel always possessed a healthy attitude towards Nazis, and to his dying day regretted that he had not killed Goebbels when he had had the opportunity.

Returning to California, Siegel found himself pitched into the roughest waters he had hitherto experienced.

Harry Greenberg was a minor mob member of Polish parentage, who was also an illegal immigrant. Deported by the American authorities, he jumped ship and found his way back to California, where he started threatening to talk to the police about the mob unless a lot of money was forthcoming. Siegel was called upon by his New York associates — men like Albert Anastasia and Buchalter — to help them to shut the mouth of the fat, overwrought Greenberg before he blabbed. Greenberg was located by a hood named Whitey Krakower, and assassins were imported from the East. But, for some unknown reason, Siegel himself — perhaps because he needed to reassert his authority in the underworld — decided to participate directly in the killing. In November 1939, Greenberg was gunned down outside his apartment. The naïve Krakower then began to talk freely about Siegel's involvement in the killing, and in July 1940 he too was found shot dead. Bugsy did not like bad publicity.

Then Abe "Kid Twist" Reles was arrested. When he turned stool-pigeon, he implicated Bugsy in the Greenberg murder, and the police felt fairly certain that they could also get him on the death of Whitey. Siegel was arrested and held in a County jail awaiting trial. This made little difference to his lifestyle. He was idolized by other inmates, who would queue up to polish his shoes. He had a specially made uniform, which another inmate regularly pressed, and he was able to order his meals from outside; roast pheasant was a particular favourite. It was election year, and Siegel was a vociferous supporter of the Democrat President, Roosevelt; he was allowed to wear a Roosevelt badge on his prison uniform. Social life presented no problems. On the pretext of visiting his dentist or conferring with his lawyer, Siegel was able to make countless trips outside prison, much to the consternation of the police, who believed they'd put him in the can and instead would come across him holding court in clubs, restaurants and movie-theatres.

In December 1940, the District Attorney dropped the charges against Siegel. The authorities now thought they had little evidence against him, but it was also murmured

that Siegel had made one or two useful contributions to the
re-election funds of certain people, and that, furthermore,
the New York authorities didn't want to risk putting Reles
in the witness stand against Siegel; they wanted to keep him
alive to testify against the big New York mafiosi.

Bugsy walked free, with all the glamour the whiff of
crime bestowed, but without the taint of a conviction. He
was considered even more desirable, and he was further
sought after by the ladies. The Hollywood stars invited this
poisonous but charming curiosity to their houses, and even
the local police developed an affection for him, often giving
him lifts back from the race track, their sirens wailing as they
escorted the cosseted gangster home. Later, when the
police thought they had more evidence against him, he
was re-arrested, but the untimely death of Kid Twist
ensured his release.

At some point in 1941 Siegel met Virginia Hill. Hill, the
daughter of poor, small-town folk from Alabama, had slept
her way across America and Mexico, marrying at least
twice, and breaking a host of hearts. She had no regard for
thrift, and spent the considerable sums of money admirers
lavished on her on lingerie and parties. One man, Joe
Epstein, a good-natured and short-sighted accountant from
Chicago with lucrative connections to a gambling syndicate, used to send her weekly packets containing wads of
thousand dollar bills; he continued to do so for years. Hill
was very beautiful: her auburn hair and grey eyes – and her
extravagant and generous personality – could reduce the
most rational of men to cringing sexual supplicants. She and
Siegel were a natural pairing. When he came calling for her
– as he did every day – she would bath in Chanel No. 5. Her
kid brother, Chick, whom she had rescued from the
drudgery of rural Alabama and took everywhere with
her, stayed on hand to provide constant room service for
the lovers. They also used a host of hotels and apartments
under a variety of pseudonyms. When the government

Naturally, Siegel wanted to be a movie star. He figured he spent all his time acting, and it seemed inevitable to him that he would one day be paid for doing so. He began turning up in the studio where George Raft was making a film with Marlene Dietrich, first watching, then going to Raft's dressing room and acting out the sequences he had witnessed. He purchased a 16mm camera, and had one of his tame hoods film his impromptu performances. He let it be known that he was interested in appearing in films and spent months trying to improve his diction and perfect his appearance. But the offers never came. He could only impersonate; he could never act.

finally went looking for Hill over a small matter of several hundred-thousand dollars in unpaid taxes, they issued a wanted poster on which they described her as a "paramour and associate of gangsters and racketeers" and gave a list of twenty aliases she had used over the years.

Hill had a wardrobe a queen would have envied: a hundred pairs of shoes, a series of $5,000 designer dresses, a dozen mink stoles, a pair of persian-lamb coats. Her winter-wear was imported from England, she had $15,000 diamond rings and each year bought herself a brand-new Cadillac. Most of the money came from Epstein. But Bugsy paid too, and put a $30,000 deposit on a house at Miami Beach for her. When questioned by the Revenue, she said that she only had an income of $16,000 a year, from betting on the horses. She did bet large sums, and won huge amounts too; but it was nothing compared to the flow of money from Epstein. Chick Hill once reckoned that his sister got through around five million dollars in these years. She didn't just spend it on herself: at times she literally threw it at people, tossing sheaves of it out of the window. No one has ever satisfactorily explained why Epstein sent her so much; some say she had a share of his gambling syndicate, others that she was one of the most successful blackmailers ever. But the truth is probably that Epstein not only was smitten, but also felt responsible for her: she became his mistress when she was only seventeen. Before her death, Hill told a friend that she hated Epstein, that he never gave her any peace, and never gave up trying to buy her back.

During the Second World War, Siegel declined to fight for his country. They probably wouldn't have let him into the Army anyway. With the nation's eyes turned outwards, he was able to expand his criminal activities, encouraging bookies to subscribe to his Trans-America race-result wire service. Most bookies already subscribed to a rival service, the Continental. But the threat of physical violence generally opened their eyes to the advantages of Siegel's wire.

He bought interests in racetracks and illegal gaming clubs in California, and, across the state line, began to acquire legitimate gambling interests in Las Vegas, where he had investments in a number of small clubs. His annual income was conservatively estimated to be around $500,000, but it was never enough. His gambling and his women saw to that, and he was forever borrowing money.

Bugsy was still married to Esta, but spent most of his time with Hill, to whom he was by no means faithful. Virginia Hill was no more faithful to Bugsy: she needed, and devoured, men but she did love Bugsy Siegel. When the attention of the police became too much for him, he decided to move out of the Hollywood mansion and escape to Nevada. Virginia was keen to get away from Hollywood too, and Bugsy even intimated that despite his need to keep up pretences of married respectability he was considering divorcing his wife. The movie star Loretta Young offered to buy his house for $85,000, but pulled out after Bugsy refused to pay $350 to have the termites in the cellar exterminated. Bugsy, irascible as ever, took her to court, lost the case, appealed and lost again. His peculiar meanness was much in evidence when he finally moved out of the house: he forced George Raft to pay him $500 for an assortment of decaying garden furniture not worth twenty dollars, which the movie star had no need for; but one didn't refuse Bugsy. "I guess he needs the money," sighed Raft, counting out the bills.

One summer day in 1945, Bugsy Siegel took his old friend Little Moe Sedway on a trip to Las Vegas, then a poky little desert town in a sea of burning sand with a collection of run-down gambling clubs. Most of the Californians who crossed the border to gamble would head for the smarter resort of Reno. Las Vegas was for ranchers, cowpokes, poor Indians and the occasional lost tourist.

Bugsy drove Moe to a remote and bleak spot seven miles outside town, where a dilapidated motel rotted in the sun. He told him his plan: he was going to buy these thirty acres of wasteland for a few cents and build a hotel and casino costing two million dollars. It would be called "Ben Siegel's Flamingo". When Moe protested at the absurdity of the idea — what possible incentive could there be for anyone to come here? — Bugsy simply stared dreamily at the desert haze and told him that one day people would drive hundreds of miles just to see the place he planned.

Fronted by his friends, Siegel bought up the land over the next few months, and floated the Nevada Projects Corporation, raising one million dollars through a share issue, all of which were bought by close associates; Meyer Lansky took shares, as did Louis Pokross, another member of the old Bug-Meyer gang. In effect, the Flamingo was financed by the Mafia. In December 1945, building began.

Bugsy was beside himself with excitement. He engaged the popular Del Webb to build the hotel, and pulled every political string he could to obtain the necessary supplies of copper, marble and steel; wartime stringencies still applied, but while veterans down the road returned from the fighting to find that they couldn't get bricks with which to build houses, the Flamingo was made a priority building project. Truly, Bugsy Siegel was a master of graft.

In the midst of this, Bugsy forgot that he hadn't seen his family for months, and Esta finally sued for a divorce from the man who was now an utter stranger, wrapped up in his twin passions of the Flamingo and Virginia Hill. She got an unusually generous settlement: Bugsy was in an ebullient mood and signed an alimony agreement worth $1,500,000 to his ex-wife.

He was being profligate on the building, too. He flew plasterers and carpenters in from other cities, and paid them fifty dollars a day. When materials weren't forthcoming, he would obtain them at extortionate prices on the black market. Lorry drivers were turning up and delivering materials which they would return at night to steal and then sell back to him the following day. He ordered that the walls be of double thickness. When it transpired that the supporting beam of the penthouse suite he intended for his own use was only going to be 5'10" off the ground and he would have to duck humbly under it every time he entered the room, he ordered this central piece of structure to be ripped out and re-designed. His vanity cost $22,500. Bugsy decided that the layout of the kitchens was wrong: it cost $30,000 to alter. Then he complained that the boiler room was too small: another $115,000. He insisted that the ninety-two bedrooms all had their private sewage systems: the plumbing bill came to $1 million. The building was his obsession, his final play for recognition; he was going to run the most glitzy hotel and casino in the country and therefore everything must be as he desired it. He was out of control.

Throughout 1946, as the hotel took shape, his temper grew fouler and his aggressive outbursts of frustration and fury more regular. He reverted to being an irascible hood, made uglier by his imperial ambitions; the workmen who battled in the sweltering Nevada heat to finish the hotel in time for a Christmas opening were afraid of his megalomania and of the boots and guns of henchmen like Hymie Segal and Little Moe Sedway. The atmosphere was fraught.

In the summer, on impulse, Bugsy and Virginia Hill flew to Mexico and were married. Siegel gave her a ruby and diamond ring. He never mentioned the wedding to anyone else; it was five years before Hill told reporters that she had once been Bugsy's wife. Bugsy was never an emotionally articulate man, and rarely expressed any sort of tenderness. But though they might not talk about it, they both knew that theirs was the love of kindred spirits. Bugsy even wrote Hill a poem once.

The Flamingo was due to open on 26 December. Realizing that the day was fast approaching, Siegel began frantically to try and publicize the hotel. He hired press agents in Los Angeles, who inundated the newspapers with photographs of the nubile beauties that would be on display at the hotel. In Las Vegas he took full page advertisements in all the region's newspapers and hired Henry Greenspun, the editor of a monthly magazine, *Las Vegas Life*, to manage his publicity (he wanted, most particularly, to ensure that he was never again known as "Bugsy"). He assiduously courted the press, sending them cases of whisky, promises of free sex at the casino and sometimes envelopes full of cash; there was many a newspaperman who disengaged himself from a firm handshake with Bugsy to find himself holding a $100 bill. He drew up a list of movie stars he wanted present for the opening and ordered Billy Wilkerson, his long-time associate in Los Angeles, to make sure they turned up and chartered a fleet of aircraft to bring them to the door of the Flamingo.

But Siegel's luck was about to run out. Randolph Hearst, the newspaper magnate, let it be known that he was none too keen on either Siegel or the Flamingo. The press kept their distance, or wrote sniping articles about Siegel's shady past. The movie stars he wanted – Joan Crawford, Spencer Tracy, Greer Garson – were advised by influential figures to stay away. In despair, Siegel contemplated cancelling the opening; but Virginia Hill had just spent $3,500 on a new dress and was not going to have her big night ruined.

On 26 December the weather was appalling. A driving wind and a foul storm kept the chartered aircraft and most of the willing celebrities grounded in Los Angeles. The spectacular ornamental waterfall outside the hotel – visible for miles – wouldn't work, because a cat had had a litter of kittens in the tap, and Siegel believed it would be bad luck to flush the kittens out. When the doors opened, it was apparent that there were more staff than customers, and only two or three names of any sort – including the faithful George Raft – had made the journey by car or train. The great occasion was a disaster.

So long as the gambling side of things could hold its own, there was hope. Casinos do have runs of bad luck, but if managed with a modicum of care, they should be money-making machines: after all, the odds are invariably in favour of the house. But Siegel was on a losing streak: the casino's losses in the first week were unprecedented. Some say that the local opposition joined up to try and bust the Flamingo in its first forty-eight hours, pouring money in to break Siegel with big early winnings. But everybody – except George Raft, who went down $65,000 on the Chemin de Fer – made a small fortune. Siegel was frantic; he switched the dice, changed the cards and moved the confused dealers from table to table. Nothing changed his luck and he was even being clipped by his own staff, who were openly playing rigged games.

After two weeks, the Flamingo had lost
$300,000. The building costs of the complex
stood at four million dollars, and there were
still ninety-two bedrooms to furnish at $3,500
each. The mob wanted to hear some good news
about their investment. Siegel was looking down
the barrel of a gun.

Siegel stalked the still unfinished hotel and casino, pumping with adrenalin, his eyes bloodshot, his temper exhausted. He began to look for fights, and tried to sock Chick Hill. He and Virginia had a vicious scrap in which she flew at him with a stiletto heel, cutting his face badly. Hill went back to Los Angeles, took a new mansion, bought new clothes and indulged herself with new lovers. She hated the desert, and was going crazy herself. One night a policeman was called to her house, to find her stalking round in her night dress, clutching a gun and announcing that she intended to kill everybody present.

Siegel's rivals in Las Vegas and Los Angeles began to spread rumours about the volcanic temper of the thug who ran the Flamingo; they said that visitors were putting their lives at risk. Finally, facing ruin, Siegel announced that he would close the Flamingo and re-open it, completely finished, in March.

He began to suspect that his backers might seriously be contemplating ridding themselves of him and might even be involved in the process of ruining him so that they could take the Flamingo over. He surrounded himself with armed hoods and lashed out wildly at anyone whom he suspected of disloyalty. He needed money so badly that he stung everyone he knew for whatever they had: George Raft was persuaded to lend him $100,000, which he never saw again.

> When the movie starlet Marie McDonald (a
> close friend of Siegel and Hill) came to Las Vegas
> they were surprised that she did not visit the
> Flamingo. She told them that the room clerk at
> her hotel, one Ray Kronsen, had flippantly said
> that the place was full of gangsters and
> murderers. Siegel was beside himself. He took
> Hymie Segal and Chick Hill and went round to
> the hotel where the clerk worked and clubbed
> him insensible with gun-butts.

The re-opening night in March was a downbeat, panicky
affair. There were no firework displays or razzmatazz, and
Siegel, his friends and their wives spent the evening running
from bedroom to bedroom, frantically trying to help the
workmen and chambermaids to finish preparing them. At
eight p.m. there were still guests in the lobby, waiting to
check into rooms that had no furniture. But, on the face of it,
business looked much better. Siegel had ridden the adverse
publicity, and people were making the trek across the desert
to visit this fabulous, glowing palace.

But Siegel's bad luck persisted. The guests were playing
in the casino, but they were still winning. The net loss for
the first six months was approaching one million dollars.
There was a series of other disasters too. On one hot
afternoon, the occupants of the swimming pool were
alarmed to see all the water disappear down a vast crack
which suddenly opened up. Many mumbled about the hand
of God and checked out immediately. It was just an
engineering flaw, and was soon repaired, but by then the
word was out: the Flamingo was cursed.

Virginia Hill was becoming more unstable. One night,
after convincing herself that Siegel was sleeping with a

blonde hat-check girl, she launched herself at the woman, and put her in hospital with a dislocated vertebra and severe facial lacerations. Siegel was furious: his arbitrary explosions were adverse publicity enough. The couple argued; Hill took an overdose. She was taken to hospital in time to save her life, but it was only the first of many suicide attempts, and one day she would succeed.

Hill was exhausted. Siegel had become a raging insomniac. He now knew that his position was hopeless, that he had insufficient experience to run the Flamingo, that his vanity and bad taste had contributed to the disaster, and that he could find no more money from anywhere. But when Hill told him to sell up and move with her, he refused.

His death was inevitable. The backers wanted him out. He had long parted company with two of the mob's contacts with the project, Gus Greenbaum and Little Moe Sedway (the man he had first taken to see the windblown, desolate site). These two seem to have been remarkably well-informed about the time-table the Mafia drew up for Bugsy's last days.

Over the few days leading up to 20 June 1947 Siegel seemed to be almost constantly on the telephone. Nobody will say who he was speaking to. Sometimes the conversations were violent disagreements, sometimes he seemed to be imploring, sometimes he was rational and friendly. On 19 June Siegel called a sidekick called Fat Irish Green into his office and showed him a briefcase containing $600,000.

"I'm going to Los Angeles for a couple of days," he said. "I want you to look after this case. If anything happens to me, just sit tight and then some guys will come and take the money off your hands."

Then he called Virginia Hill's house on Linden Drive in Los Angeles. He got hold of Chick and told him that he would be over that night, accompanied by his associate, Alan Smiley. He said that he was going to have a meeting at his lawyer's the next day.

He arrived, slept, had his meeting and then went to a barber's and had a leisurely lunch. He also had a talk with an old mob friend, Mickey Cohen, and asked him if he could get hold of some guys with "equipment". Cohen dropped a couple of names, and Siegel said he'd see them the following day. To Cohen, it looked as if Siegel was even now planning to fight back. After dinner at Jack's Restaurant in Ocean Park, Siegel and Smiley returned to Linden Drive. Siegel opened the door with the solid gold key that Virginia had given him, and he and Smiley sat in the lounge, which was decorated in a curious mixture of English chintz and American camp, talking over the grim state of business.

At 10.20 p.m. on 20 June 1947, as the two men talked, Chick was upstairs, fumbling with the clothing of his girlfriend Jerri Mason. Suddenly, he heard what sounded like gunfire downstairs. When he reached the lounge, Al Smiley screamed at him to turn the lights out. He did so, and both men stood in the dark, trembling, with Jerri Mason screaming in the background. They heard a car pull away. After a while, they switched the lights back on. Chick saw that Smiley was hiding in the fireplace, and on the floor, his head nearly severed by nine shots from a .30-30 carbine, was the corpse of Benjamin "Bugsy" Siegel. His right eye was found plastered to the ceiling fifteen feet away, and his eyelids with their luxuriant lashes were glued to an adjoining door jamb.

The front-facing window of the lounge was shattered by bullets. The killer had come very close to the house, and had carefully rested his gun on the tasteful lattice-work frame that shielded the house from the road. Siegel had been a sitting target because, curiously, the curtains had been open, as if by arrangement.

Within twenty minutes of his death, Greenbaum and Moe Sedway strolled through the doors of the Flamingo and took control of the complex. Later, a group of

Little Moe Sedway died of multiple ailments and was buried in the same cemetery not fifty feet from Siegel, his bitter enemy. Gus Greenbaum was not so fortunate: he fell out with his Mafia masters and in 1958 was decapitated with a butcher's knife while asleep in Las Vegas; his wife was then knifed and strangled for good measure as she lay beside him.

businessmen called on Fat Irish Green, and relieved him of the cash that Bugsy had deposited with him. The Flamingo was refinanced, and given a respectable front man. In a short time, it began to make vast profits, and all along the bleak road where it had once stood as a lonely memorial to the grandiose dreams of a dead mobster sprang up a host of other, glittering gambling palaces. The modern city of Las Vegas was born.

Siegel had a handsome coffin, made of scrolled silver and bronze and lined with silk, costing $5,000. Few of his associates attended the funeral; the police and press outnumbered the mourners. Virginia Hill didn't come, nor did George Raft, nor the Countess DiFrasso. Just his family — his ex-wife, his daughters, his sister.

Virginia Hill was in Paris when Siegel was killed. She checked out of her hotel and drove to Monaco, where she sat alone in the Casino. Later that night she took an overdose of barbiturates. She survived, then returned to Paris where she took a suite in the Ritz and again tried to kill herself. She flew back to America, but the pattern of attempted suicide persisted. On each occasion she was saved only by fortunate intervention, mostly by Chick. Pursued by the Internal Revenue and eaten by depression and loneliness, she finally fled the United States and made her way, via Mexico, to Europe.

Gangsters

Hill went to live in the ski resort of Klosters, outside Zurich. She was increasingly unstable, and regularly assaulted her brother's girlfriends (throughout her life she possessed a formidable right jab). Before leaving America she had married Hans Hauser, an Austrian-born ski-instructor reputed to have the looks and body of Apollo. She even had a child, Peter, by him. But she was never happy with Hans, and soon despised him. The Revenue had already seized everything she owned in the US – her house, her cars, her mink coats. Now she tried to strike a deal with them. She would come back, try and settle her tax and serve a nominal sentence. But the deal fell apart. She lurched on: to Salzburg, then Prague and then Cuba, from where she was immediately sent back to Prague (she was unaware that Castro was now in power). Epstein stopped sending her money; she was broke, and raged against the world.

Finally, in March 1966, Hill drove to the small, beautiful mountain village of Koppl outside Salzburg and, by a waterfall, swallowed twenty-eight barbiturates and quietly died. She was forty-nine years old.

Chapter Five

AL CAPONE: PUBLIC ENEMY NUMBER ONE

C ontrary to popular belief, Al "Scarface" Capone, the most infamous of the Chicago gangsters, was unconnected to the Mafia. He was not a Sicilian, and he spent his active life quarrelling with the "Mob". Capone came from a Neapolitan family and was born in Brooklyn in 1899, the fourth son of Gabriele and Teresa Capone, who had emigrated from Naples some six years previously. Like all gangsters, he was involved in crime from an early age, running with the so-called "Five Points Gang", which was led by another Italian, John Torrio, a future partner in violence. At the age of fifteen, young Alphonse discovered that The Black Hand, a Camorra/Mafia murder squad, was extorting money from his father. He tracked down the two men responsible, shooting them dead. Torrio was impressed.

In 1919 the Volsted Act was passed, and America began its long and ultimately disastrous experiment with Prohibition. Torrio had been in Chicago for a few years already, establishing himself as a serious gangster. In Chicago, illegal drinkers were kept supplied by one of a dozen big gangs, each of which had its own clearly defined territory. Torrio controlled the South Side of the city, in conjunction with the Irish Duggan-Lake gang who supplied the Inner West Side. The rest of the West Side was run by the Genna brothers, Sicilians from Marsala, who were noted for the pleasure they derived from killing. The North Side of Chicago was the province of Dion O'Banion, a small time thief who ran a flower shop opposite the Holy Name Cathedral. He worked in conjunction with two Poles, George "Bugs" Moran and Hymie Weiss.

At first there was little trouble between the gangs; there was enough business to go around, and the gangs' energies were devoted towards organizing themselves into efficient units. But within a year, they began to look for opportunities to muscle in on each others' profits, and the murders began. Torrio suddenly acquired rivals on the South Side, the O'Donnell gang, who started hijacking his beer trucks and smashing up his drinking dens. He had several of their drivers killed, but he realized that in the circumstances attack was the best form of defence. If he did not exert control over the whole of Chicago, it was unlikely that he would survive at all. He needed skilled, violent men who were prepared to kill without remorse and casting his mind back he remembered the young Capone, now twenty-one and a lieutenant in the Five Points Gang. Torrio lured him to Chicago with an extraordinary offer: Capone would get twenty-five per cent of all existing turnover and fifty per cent of any further business.

Within two years Capone had gained control of the middle class Chicago suburb of Cicero, which became his personal headquarters. The local police and town authorities were in his pocket, and through the classic mix of bribery and intimidation his illegal casinos, brothels and bars were left alone to flourish. He also killed in public with impunity. Nobody would testify against him and he and Torrio were raking in $100,000 a week apiece.

Both Torrio and Capone agreed that absolute control of Chicago was there for the taking but Capone, no diplomat, wanted to shoot his way to the top in an all-out gang war; Torrio was more circumspect and tried to persuade his irascible partner to bide his time. Then, in October 1924, a

One of Capone's first victims in Chicago was Joe Howard, a small time crook, who unwisely stole two consignments of Torrio's alcohol. The following night, as he sat enjoying the "happy hour" in his neighbourhood drinking hole, Capone walked in and shot him six times at point-blank range in front of a gallery of witnesses. The police arrested Capone, but had to release him when, after a series of personal visits from smartly-dressed men in large cars, all the witnesses became uncertain as to what, if anything, they had seen.

dispute broke out between the Gennas and the O'Banion gang. The Sicilians had stolen a cargo of the Irishman's whisky. O'Banion swore revenge, but on 4 November was himself mown down in his flower shop by three men posing as customers. The murder was almost certainly the work of Capone and Torrio, but both they and the Gennas had convenient alibis, and although the street outside the shop had been crowded, once again no one had heard or seen anything. The coroner was forced to return a verdict of "unlawful killing at the hands of a person or persons unknown".

O'Banion had a lavish funeral. His body lay in state at the undertakers for three days. Silver angels stood at the head and feet of his corpse, bearing in their hands ten candles that burned in solid gold candlesticks. Mounted police had to maintain order as the vast procession wound its way to the cemetery; there were twenty-six trucks of floral tributes, valued at $50,000. Capone sent a bunch of red roses, with a dedication: "from Al". Both he and Torrio attended the funeral.

Gangsters

Capone was now a pillar of the establishment, most of which was on his payroll (it is thought that he spent some thirty million dollars annually on back-handers and bribes and blatantly bought favourable politicians, financing the re-election campaign of Mayor "Big Bill" Thompson to the tune of $260,000). A conservative man, strong on family values, he dressed immaculately, in hand-made silk shirts, and sported diamond tie-pins. He gave generously to charities, and church restoration funds. He contributed $100,000 to a fund for striking miners, and during the Depression opened a string of soup kitchens and gave more than two million dollars to help ease the plight of the poor. When an old woman was blinded in the cross-fire of an assassination attempt on him, he paid $10,000 to have her sight restored.

O'Banion's organization was taken over by Hymie Weiss, his trusted lieutenant. Weiss adored O'Banion, and wept buckets by his grave. He swore revenge and a few days later Capone's car was swept by machine-gun fire. He escaped unhurt, but Torrio was not so lucky: two weeks later he was gunned down by another of the late O'Banion's men, Bugs Moran, in front of his wife. He recovered, but soon found himself in jail on charges of operating an illegal brewery. In prison, his nerve began to crack. He had steel screens fitted to the windows of his cell and paid for three extra sheriffs to stand guard; he wanted out of Chicago. In 1925, on his release from prison, he announced he was leaving town. Chicago, he said, was "too violent". At the age of forty-eight, Torrio took retirement and Capone, then only twenty-six, inherited his criminal empire. Shortly after his ascent to power, three of the six Genna brothers — Angel, Mike and Antonio — died in gun-battles. The others decided that life in Sicily was preferable to death in America, and retired hastily to Marsala. Only Weiss and Bugs Moran now stood between Capone and absolute control of Chicago.

Weiss fought back in spectacular style. In broad daylight, no less than eight car-loads of his henchmen descended on Capone's headquarters at the Hawthorne Inn and within the space of a few seconds they pumped over a thousand bullets into the building. Capone escaped, but decided to bring the dispute to a swift conclusion and on 11 October 1926 Hymie Weiss was gunned down on the steps of Holy Name Cathedral. Ten days later, Capone called a meeting of the Chicago gang leaders. "We're a bunch of saps to be killing each other" he told them. They nodded their assent, and agreed to a peaceful carve-up of the whole of Cook County.

For a while there was peace, and everybody made money. Capone became fabulously wealthy. Within Cook County he controlled no less than 10,000 illegal drinking dens, or speakeasies, each of which purchased an average of six barrels of beer and two cases of liquor a week from him. The beer reputedly brought him about three and a half million dollars a week; the liquor another one point eight million. When the proceeds from his gambling and prostitution rackets were added to this, his income was estimated at six and a half million dollars a week. Though his overheads were vast, his profits still made him a multi-millionaire.

Capone thought that Chicago was no place to bring up his children. By 1928, he felt secure enough about his position to look around for a second home, somewhere away from the city. Not every state was keen on having him as a resident. He was thrown out of California, and tried

Florida instead. Its citizens objected vociferously, but Capone succeeded in buying a palatial residence on Palm Island, Miami, where he quietly passed Christmas and New Year of 1929.

While he was away, Bugs Moran, the man who had shot Torrio in revenge for the murder of O'Banion, decided to settle his long-standing score with Capone. He began to muscle in on Capone's activities, regularly stealing his consignments of liquor, and threatening the other, more legitimate businesses that Capone had poured his illicit wealth into. When the source of the trouble became apparent, Capone acted swiftly. He called his right-hand man, Jake Guzik, and gave orders for the elimination of Moran. The time and place of the killing were fixed: it was to be 10.30 a.m. on 14 February 1929, St Valentine's day.

On that cold and grey Chicago morning, six of Moran's men — and one other man, an optician called Doctor Richard Schwimmer, whose presence has never been explained — were standing nonchalantly in a garage on North Clark Street, waiting for a truck-load of stolen whisky to arrive. Shortly after 10.30 a.m., a local resident, Mrs Max Landeman, heard the sound of shots coming from the adjoining garage. Looking out of the window, she saw a man leave the garage and get into a large black touring car. Another woman, Miss Josephine Morin, who lived in the flat below, saw two men come out of the garage with their hands raised above their heads. They were followed by two uniformed police officers, who had their guns drawn. She presumed she was witnessing an arrest. The four men got into a large black Cadillac and drove off.

Curiosity got the better of Mrs Landeman, and she hurried over to the garage. The doors were shut. Pushing them open, she saw seven men piled in a bloody heap on the floor. In addition to the optician, the bodies were later identified as being those of Frank and Peter Gusenberg, Moran's principal hit-men; James Clark, Moran's brother-in-law; Al Weinshank,

Captured booze during the Prohibition — 1921

Chicago cops with armoured car

Capone came back from Florida in high spirits, only to discover that two of his trusted lieutenants, John Scalise and Albert Anselmi, had ambitions to take over the "outfit". Capone organized a communal gang meal, inviting the two to join him and other favourites in a private room at a restaurant in Hammond, Indiana. To those present, Al Capone seemed in an uncommonly good mood. He laughed and joked and kept the drink flowing. Then, towards the end of the meal, he got up and sauntered around to where Scalise and Anselmi were seated. Leaning over the backs of their chairs, he smiled sweetly at them. "I hear you boys want my job," he said. "Well come and get it!", Picking up a baseball bat that was positioned on an adjoining table, he smashed in their skulls.

his accountant; Adam Heyer, his business-manager; and Johnny May, a burglar. It looked as if Capone's men had entered, disguised as policemen, lined them up facing the wall and then massacred them. Frank Gusenberg was still alive when the police arrived. They tried to persuade him to talk, but he refused to say who the killers had been. He died three hours after entering hospital, without breaking the gangster's sacred code of silence.

Bugs Moran was lucky. He should have been with his men, but had been unexpectedly delayed. By the time he arrived, it was all over; he saw the police cars and ambulances and made himself scarce. He had no doubts about who had ordered the killing: only Al Capone would contemplate such a massacre. At the time of the shooting, Capone was in the office of a Miami official, arguing about

Al Capone winks at the camera as he arrives at the Chicago Courthouse prior to being sentenced to 11 years in prison and a £10,000 fine for tax evasion

his right to reside in Florida. The police picked up some other members of his gang, but they too had alibis. Jack "Machine-Gun" MacGurn, Capone's prize executioner, claimed to have been with his girlfriend at the time of the killing, and even married her so that she could not be forced to testify against him. In the end no one was ever charged in connection with the St Valentine's Day Massacre, but Moran was finished as a force.

Gang members began to whisper that there was something a little unstable about Capone. His temper had become shorter, his use of violence less selective. The killings grew indiscriminate, and men from all walks of life were gunned down, knifed and garrotted for the most petty of offences.

In the spring of 1929, Capone found himself under unusual pressure. Herbert Hoover had been elected President, and had promised the nation an onslaught against organized crime, naming Al Capone Public Enemy Number One. In addition, Capone discovered that there was a highly enticing contract out on his life. Its possible source was Moran, but it might just as easily have emanated from the families of Scalise and Anselmi, or one of the hundreds of others whose relatives had been destroyed by Capone; even his own men thought that he was becoming a liability.

Capone decided to drop out of circulation for a while, and contrived to have himself arrested for a minor firearms offence. He expected thirty quiet and safe days in jail, but was horrified to find that he had been put away for a whole year. It made little difference to his life, as he soon managed to establish good links with his Chicago operations, and continued to control events from the security of his prison cell.

Meanwhile, Hoover embarked on a series of meetings with various arms of his administration: the Prohibition Bureau, the FBI and the Treasury Department. The officials discussed how they might be able to put Capone away permanently. Since Capone had most of the police in his pocket it was impossible to find witnesses to his crimes and orthodox methods were unlikely to succeed. For a while the Justice Department launched an all-out war on his organization, smashing up his breweries and trucks, but it had little long-term effect: Capone had the resources to absorb the attacks and come back.

By far the most successful department in the fight against organized crime was the Treasury. Frank Wilson, the senior investigator of their Special Intelligence Unit, had already succeeded in putting away a number of Capone's associates, including Frank Nitti (his deputy), Jack Guzik (his accountant), and his brother Ralph; all got sentences of between eighteen months and five years.

Since Capone had no bank account in his own name, and all his assets nominally belonged to others, Wilson had little to go on. He would have to prove that Capone's lavish lifestyle indicated undeclared income and unpaid taxes.

Gangsters can't declare the source of their earnings and have a natural aversion to paying taxes. Capone claimed that he lived off $450 a month; because his earnings were therefore less than $5,000 a year, he had never filed a tax-return.

Wilson began piecing together the record of Capone's personal spending. He found that between 1926 and 1929 Capone had purchased more then $25,000 of furniture for his various homes; he had also spent $7,000 on suits and another $40,000 on telephone calls. In all, Wilson found that in that period Capone had spent some $165,000, which clearly indicated undeclared income. It would only be enough to put Capone away for three years; they needed more. Finally Wilson persuaded some of Capone's casino employees to talk, and the Treasury was able to charge Capone with failing to pay taxes on one million dollars of undeclared earnings, meriting a possible thirty years in prison.

At first Capone's attorney struck a deal with the prosecution: if his client pleaded guilty he would get no more than two years in prison. But when the Judge heard about the arrangement he was disgusted and refused to accept it.

Capone went on trial. The jurors were subject to persistent threats and attempts at bribery, which necessitated a last minute change of the entire jury. On 24 October 1931, Capone was found guilty on all counts and was sentenced to eleven years in prison and fined $50,000, the most severe sentence ever imposed for a tax offence. He was imprisoned in Cook County jail while his lawyers lodged an appeal. It failed, and in May 1932 he was shipped to Atlanta Federal Penitentiary and from there he was moved to the infamous prison on Alcatraz in San Francisco Bay.

Shortly after he began his sentence, Capone was diagnosed as suffering from syphilis. All attempts at a cure failed and by the time he was released in 1939 the disease had reached its debilitating tertiary stage: at the age of thirty-eight, Al Capone was going mad. He went to live at his home on Palm Island, Florida. Surrounded by his family, and under constant medical supervision, he survived for another seven years, a grim, haunted figure, his mind slowly consumed by syphilis. In 1947 he died following a brain haemorrhage and his body was returned to Chicago, the scene of his triumphs, where he was buried, at great cost, in a marble mausoleum in the cemetery at Mount Olive.

Chapter Six

WAS DILLINGER SHOT?

Towards the end of his short life, John Herbert Dillinger was designated "public enemy number one", a distinction he shared with hold-up men like Baby Face Nelson, Pretty Boy Floyd and "Bonnie and Clyde". According to police records, Dillinger's sudden and violent end occurred outside the Biograph cinema in Chicago on 22 July 1934, when he was shot down by FBI agents. But since then there have been frequent doubts expressed about whether the man who died was actually the famous gangster.

John Herbert Dillinger was born on 22 June 1903, the product of an unhappy home life. When he was in sixth grade at school he was charged with stealing coal from the Pennsylvania Railroad's wagons to sell to residents of his Indianapolis neighbourhood. An angry magistrate shouted at him, "Your mind is crippled!"

When his father bought a small farm outside Mooresville, Indiana, Dillinger found country life intolerable. When a love affair went wrong he stole a car, drove to Indianapolis, and enlisted in the US Navy. During his four months as a sailor he was AWOL several times, and finally deserted in December. Back in Indiana, he married a sixteen-year-old girl and moved in with her parents. One day, after drinking in a pool hall, Dillinger and a former convict named Edgar Singleton concocted a robbery plan. They attacked a Mooresville grocer with a baseball bat, but the grocer fought back so vigorously that the would-be bandits fled. Dillinger was arrested on suspicion. When his father

John Dillinger.

arrived at the gaol he admitted to the robbery, and the prosecutor promised his father that his son would receive a lenient sentence if he threw himself on the mercy of the court. It was Dillinger's bad luck to be brought before a severe judge, who fined him $200 and sentenced him to from ten to twenty years. Outraged at the broken promise, Dillinger made several unsuccessful attempts to escape from the State Reformatory at Pendleton. He also came under the influence of two determined bank robbers – Harry Pierpont and Homer Van Meter. Dillinger, who had homosexual tendencies, also had a lover in prison.

Released in May 1933, after a petition from the residents of Mooresville, Dillinger set out to organize a mass escape for his former friends, who were then in the state prison in Michigan City. He began committing a series of bank robberies, in one of them netting $10,600. But a girl cashier in a bank at Daleville, Indiana, told the police that she felt that Dillinger – who wore a straw boater to commit the robbery – was anxious not to frighten her. His sense of impudent humour revealed itself when, in the World Fair in Chicago in the summer of 1933, he asked a policeman if he would snap a picture of himself and of his girlfriend Mary Longnaker.

In September 1933 Dillinger tossed three guns wrapped in newspapers into the athletic field at Michigan City prison, but other inmates found them and handed them over to the Warden. Next, Dillinger bribed the foreman of a thread-making company to conceal loaded guns in a barrel that was being sent to the shirt shop in the prison. But by the time his friends broke out of gaol Dillinger was already back in custody again – police keeping a watch on his girlfriend Mary had succeeded in arresting him. Ten men escaped. Shortly after, they rescued Dillinger from the Lima gaol, killing Sheriff Jess Sarber in the process. Eight days later, Dillinger and Pierpont walked into the gaol at Peru, Indiana, explained that they were tourists, and asked the

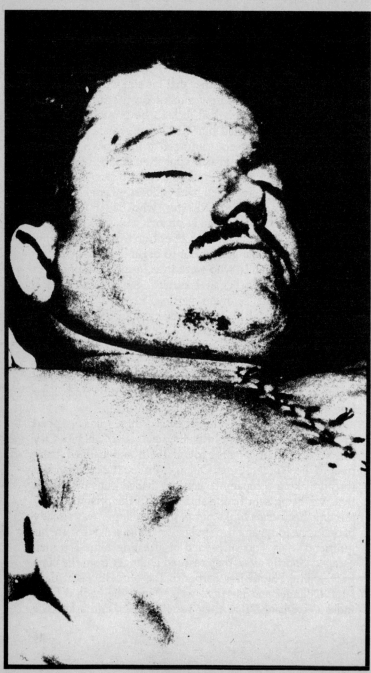

The man believed to be John Dillinger – in the morgue.

For a brief period in the 1920s, the gang led by brothers Matt and George Kimes and Ray Terrill was one of the most successful in America. The members were all farm boys, many of whom had decided that bootlegging was more profitable than ploughing.

Terrill persuaded the Kimes brothers that bank robbery would be even more profitable than bootlegging, and so it proved. A raid at the Farmer's National Bank in Beggs, Oklahoma, netted $20,000. They were captured when their car hit a tree but Terrill and Matt Kimes escaped and robbed the same bank again, this time taking $18,000.

In Pampa, Texas, in 1927, the gang learned that the huge old iron bank safe was almost uncrackable, so they rolled it outside – while customers were held up by other gang members – loaded it on to a truck and drove away with it. It proved to contain $35,000.

Matt Kimes was caught soon after this and sentenced to life. Terrill teamed up with Herman Barker, eldest of Ma Barker's sons, but in September 1927, after a shoot-out during which they escaped, Barker was found dead in a ditch. (Ma Barker always claimed he had been "executed" by the police.) Terrill was captured soon after and spent most of his life behind bars.

police chief what precautions they had taken against the Dillinger gang. The police showed them their arsenal; Dillinger and Pierpont produced their guns, and left town

The police officers who aided in the capture of the notorious Dillinger gang

with a car full of machine guns, shotguns and bullet-proof vests.

Now the "Dillinger mob" (as the press had already dubbed them) committed a whole series of robberies — the exact number is not certain — which made them notorious. When Dillinger was in a bank in Greencastle, Indiana, he saw a farmer standing at the counter with a pile of money in front of him. He asked, "Is that your money or the bank's?" "Mine," the farmer said. "Keep it," said Dillinger, and walked out with his sack full of the bank's cash. This kind of story brought Dillinger a reputation as a modern Robin Hood. The robbery brought the gang over $75,000. That winter they decided to move down to a warmer climate, and drove to Daytona Beach, Florida. But when they moved to Tucson, Arizona, their luck ran out: a fire broke out in their hotel, and a fireman discovered that their cases contained guns and ammunition. They were arrested and sent back to Indiana. Pierpont was charged with killing Sheriff Sarber.

On 3 March 1934 Dillinger made his spectacular escape from Crown Point gaol, Indiana, with a wooden gun that he had carved with a razor. The escape made him famous. (In fact, later investigation showed that Dillinger had somehow managed to get a real gun from somewhere.) Two weeks after the escape, Dillinger's fellow-escapee, Herbert Youngblood, was killed in a battle with police. Dillinger quickly organized another gang, including Homer Van Meter and the short-tempered Baby Face Nelson (real name Lester Gillis). He also sent money for Pierpont's defence, but it did no good — Pierpont and another accomplice died in the electric chair. Soon after this Dillinger himself narrowly escaped death in a gun battle with police in St Paul, Minnesota. A month later police closed in around Dillinger's hideout at Little Bohemia Lodge, near Rhinelander, Wisconsin, but again the gang escaped. Only some innocent bystanders were shot. (The comedian Will Rogers

The 1930s outlaws took to Tommy guns like children with a brand-new toy. Dillinger posed with one of his in photographs, while "Pretty Boy" Floyd preferred more practical displays, stripping his weapon of buttstock and foregrip to create a kind of super-pistol. George "Machine Gun" Kelly liked to practise on walnuts, while "Baby Face" Nelson preferred human targets, mowing down two FBI agents in November 1934. (One of the G-men had a Thompson, too, and Nelson was hit seventeen times before he collapsed. His final words – "I think I'm hit" – remain an all-time classic understatement.)

Still, for all their fabled firepower, Tommy guns had certain shortcomings. Texas lawman Ted Hinton, shooting it out with Clyde Barrow and Bonnie Parker in 1933, watched his .45 rounds bouncing off the outlaw vehicle. Disgusted, Hinton shifted his allegiance to the mighty Browning Automatic Rifle, backing it up with a shotgun and two .45 Colts when he helped ambush Bonnie and Clyde a year later. (Barrow and John Paul Chase – a sidekick of Baby Face Nelson – also favoured the BAR for running shootouts, but other outlaws rejected the piece as too heavy and awkward.)

joked that the only way Dillinger would get shot was if he got among some innocent bystanders some time.)

Under a plastic surgery operation to alter his face, Dillinger almost died, but the surgeon managed to pull his tongue out of his throat and got him breathing again.

With his new face, Dillinger had the confidence to go out into the open again. In Chicago he began to date a waitress named Polly Hamilton. Polly's room-mate was a forty-two-year-old woman called Anna Sage, who had served time for running a brothel. Anna was under threat of deportation, and when she learned Dillinger's identity it struck her that she might persuade the authorities to lift the deportation order if she betrayed him. Dillinger was now using the name James Lawrence.

So it came about that on the evening of 22 July 1934 Dillinger took his girlfriend Polly and Anna Sage to the Biograph cinema to see *Manhattan Melodrama*, starring Clark Gable. Anna Sage was wearing a bright red dress, in order to be easily identifiable. As they came out of the cinema FBI agent Melvin Purvis approached him and challenged him. The gangster pulled a Colt automatic from his pocket and sprinted for the nearest alleyway. Three agents fired, and Dillinger fell dead, with a bullet through his left eye; the man who had fired it was police detective Martin Zarkovich, of East Chicago. Later that day newsmen were taken to the morgue to see Dillinger's body. Foreign correspondent Negley Farson tells how the policeman pulled back the sheet over the naked body, and said grinning: "Well hung, isn't he?"

But was it Dillinger? The autopsy notes – made by Dr J.J. Kearns, the Cook County chief pathologist – reveal that the corpse's eyes were brown. Dillinger's were blue. The dead man possessed a rheumatic heart condition, chronic since childhood. Dillinger did not – he would not have been allowed to join the navy if he had. Lawrence was shorter and heavier than Dillinger, and had none of the scars and wounds or birthmarks that Dillinger was known to have.

Crime writer Jay Robert Nash has argued that the FBI was duped into believing that the dead man was Dillinger, and that J. Edgar Hoover was too embarrassed to admit the mistake afterwards. "Jimmy Lawrence", according to Nash, was a small-time hoodlum, who came from Wisconsin to Chicago about 1930 and was often seen in the neighbourhood of the Biograph cinema. If Nash is correct, then we may assume that the "lady in red" deliberately "set up" the small-time hoodlum in a plot to provide Dillinger with a permanent escape. A photograph taken from the handbag of Dillinger's girlfriend Billie Frechette some time before his "killing" shows her with a man who bears an amazing resemblance to the corpse of James Lawrence. It seems possible, therefore, that she was also involved in the plot to take the heat off her former lover.

Within months Dillinger's gang was wiped out. Homer Van Meter was killed in an alley and Baby Face Nelson died in a gun battle, after killing two FBI agents. Harry Pierpont attempted to escape from the death house in the Ohio State Prison by carving a gun out of soap, but the ruse failed. He was electrocuted in October 1934.

What happened to Dillinger? A fellow-gangster, Blackie Audett, who claims to have been in the Biograph cinema that evening, asserts in his book *Wrapsheet* that Dillinger married and fled to Oregon. He "disappeared" in the 1940s.

Chapter Seven

BONNIE AND CLYDE: DEPRESSION MOBSTERS

During the drab, poverty-stricken years of the Great Depression, the Great Plains became the hunting ground for a number of celebrated gangsters who specialized in motorized crime. Although criminals like any others, their poor backgrounds and their reputation for robbing banks rather than other struggling individuals gave them the image of latter-day Robin Hoods. As much as anything, the stories of their doomed and violent lives made good news in an otherwise dull decade.

Foremost amongst them were the young lovers Bonnie Parker and Clyde Barrow, now folk heroes and the subject of many works of fiction. In reality they were a little less scrupulous about killing than the legends suggest. Clyde Barrow, who was born on 24 March 1909 into an impoverished Texan farming family, had a particularly vicious streak, and it was claimed that from an early age he took great pleasure in torturing farm animals.

His future partner, Bonnie Parker, two years his junior, came from a devout Baptist environment. Her father died when she was four and the family moved to the gruesomely named Cement City, Texas. A pretty, petite blonde, Bonnie was much sought after and when only sixteen married a Dallas bum named Roy Thornton. He was soon in jail, doing life for murder, and at the age of nineteen she met the handsome, polite and pleasant Clyde, whom her mother

Bonnie Parker

thought a lovely boy. Her illusions were shattered when Clyde was arrested on seven counts of burglary and car theft. But her daughter was smitten and helped Clyde to escape from jail, smuggling in a gun. A few days later he was picked up again, this time for robbing a railway ticket-office at gunpoint, and sentenced to fourteen years in a grim Texas prison.

There was nothing Bonnie could do this time, so Clyde got to thinking and came up with the ingenious idea of persuading another inmate to cut off two of his toes with an axe. Thus crippled, he was deemed to have suffered enough, and released. He hobbled straight back to Bonnie. He tried going straight, but the work was dull, the pay bad and you still died at the end of it all. Crime held less prospect of such prolonged disappointment. He and Bonnie headed for West Dallas; they picked up a friend of Clyde's, one Ray Hamilton, acquired two other gang members and hit the road.

They rarely struck gold – the biggest haul was a mere $3,500 – and after a few minor heists Clyde committed his first murder, when he shot a jeweller in Hillsboro, Texas. They got away with the grand total of forty dollars. Bonnie was in custody at the time, on suspicion of auto-theft. By the time she was released, three months later, the gang had signed their death warrants by gunning down a Sheriff and his Deputy outside a Texas dance hall.

Some of their murders were the result either of a surprisingly casual attitude to killing or of sheer nerves; little else could explain the occasion on which Bonnie shot a Texas butcher three times in the stomach, or the unnecessary death of the son of a car owner whose vehicle they were stealing. The police stalked them relentlessly. In 1933, they went to hide out in Missouri, where they were joined by Clyde's hitherto respectable brother, Buck, and his neurotic wife, Blanche. Such a large group made it all the easier for the police to find them. They were duly

> "Pretty Boy" Floyd was so christened by an
> affectionate whorehouse madam in Kansas City.
> Named Charles Arthur, he was a tall and
> muscular farm labourer from Oklahoma who
> one day tossed aside his shovel and decided on a
> career as a gangster. A contemporary of Bonnie
> and Clyde, he ploughed exactly the same
> furrow, robbing banks and shooting anyone who
> opposed him. Caught and sentenced to fifteen
> years for the one killing they could pin on him,
> Pretty Boy hopped off the train taking him to
> prison and went back to work. He was finally
> gunned down by the FBI in Ohio in 1934.

surrounded but, by now heavily armed, they shot their way
out, killing two policemen.

On the run, the two became increasingly morbid; aware
that they would inevitably die, they were concerned that
they would never see their parents again. A certain
desperation crept into their behaviour, and the killings
became even more arbitrary. They survived a nasty car
crash, and escaped again from a police assault, before they
were once more cornered in Missouri. Again they managed
to escape, but this time the police scored: Buck was shot in
the head, and Blanche was blinded. Bonnie was still crippled
from the car crash. When Clyde stopped driving to buy
water and food, the police were on them. Buck was riddled
with bullets and died in hospital six days later. Blanche
stayed with her dead husband, and was sentenced to ten
years in prison.

Bonnie and Clyde eluded the authorities for the next
three months. Betrayed by a former gang member, the
police staked them out and ambushed their car as they

returned from shopping. On 23 May 1934 the Ford V8 sedan they were driving had nearly a hundred rounds pumped into it. They died instantly, very young and very pretty. When they were buried in Dallas, they pulled crowds from all over the country.

Chapter Eight

ÉMILE THE NUT AND JACQUES MESRINE

Émile the Nut

Across the Atlantic, gangsters in Paris and Marseilles were studying the exploits of their American counterparts with admiration. One of these was perhaps France's most notorious and dangerous gangster since the far-off days of the Bonnot gang: Émile Buisson.

Buisson's heredity seems to have been extremely bad. His father was a drunkard, a builder of bakers' ovens, addicted to absinthe. Only four of his nine children survived, and one of them was a weak-minded deaf-mute girl. The two criminals of the family, Jean-Baptiste and Émile, were its only two healthy members; a third brother died of tuberculosis at the age of twenty. The mother, worn out by overwork, starvation, and continual brutal beatings from her husband, was taken to an asylum. The father took to exhibiting his deaf-mute daughter in cafés for money; he was sent to jail for carnal knowledge of minors — including his daughter — and died in an asylum.

Émile was born at Paray-le-Monial, in the Sâone-et-Loire department of southern France, on 19 August 1902. His elder brother fought in the war, deserted, and was sent to a penal battalion in Algeria. Released in 1921, he promptly became a pimp in Paris.

Émile served his first term in jail at the age of sixteen, and then twenty months' imprisonment for theft. He was due for military service, and so sent out to a penal battalion in

Albert Spaggiari had been a hired gun for a right-wing terrorist organisation and had served in the paratroopers in French Indochina. By 1976, however, he was running a photographic supply shop in Nice, ostensibly a settled man. Yet he was planning one of the biggest and most daring bank robberies ever.

The Société Générale Bank in Nice had an ancient vault, built in the 1900s, and Spaggiari knew that this made it a relatively easy target. He surveyed the bank for hours, looking for a way to get to the vault without having to go through the modern building above ground. One day he saw his chance: a team of city cleaners were leaving the sewer from a manhole in a direct line with the vault. If he could tunnel through the underground masonry into the bank while the vault was locked, he could loot the safe deposit boxes and bullion almost at his leisure.

He recruited accomplices of equally dubious backgrounds, including Gaby Anglade, who in 1962 had tried to assassinate Charles De Gaulle, and Jean Kay, a conman who once cheated a rich industrialist out of 8,000,000 francs.

The tunnel was started in an underground parking facility opposite the bank, and took two months to complete. The diggers worked by the light of a fluorescent strip light attached to half a mile of cable, and Spaggiari catered the excavations, regularly bringing large amounts of food and wine down into the tunnel for his partners.

The tunnel complete, the robbery was carried off on 20 July 1976, France's Independence holiday. The gang moved sixty million francs in cash, bonds and jewellery from the vault, leaving the vault's doors welded shut to delay discovery of the crime. Supposedly the gang found some pornographic photographs belonging to a blackmailer in one of the deposit boxes, and pinned them up all around the vault. They also left a message that read: "Without weapons, without hate and without violence."

By October the police had found some of the stolen bonds being sold by a garage owner in Nice. Following this lead, they arrested Spaggiari at Nice Côte d'Azur airport, where he had just returned from a holiday in New York, Hong Kong and Bangkok.

He remained in custody for only four months. Expecting a fifteen to twenty year jail sentence, he broke free of the court security and dived through a loosely secured window onto the street below. As his defence lawyer shouted: "No! not that!" he was picked up by a waiting motorcyclist and driven to freedom.

North Africa. The brutality of these battalions was unspeakable. However, Émile managed to distinguish himself in the fighting, and got the Croix de Guerre. Back in France, he took up a life of petty crime and served many short terms in jail.

In 1932, he helped to rescue his brother from jail. The plan was bold. Jean-Baptiste got himself transferred to Strasbourg model prison at Ensisheim by confessing to a crime in Strasbourg and getting three years added to his eight-year sentence. He there broke his leg by smashing it with a table leg. He was transferred into the hospital, and the same night jumped from a first-floor window, breaking it again. However, with the help of Émile he made a clean getaway.

Émile Buisson committed his first big robbery on 27 December 1937, and got himself the nickname "Mimile le Dingue" – Crazy Mimile. He was driving a "traction avant" Citröen – front-wheel drive (known generally simply as "tractions"), and he and a gangster named Charles Desgrandschamps (known as "Bigfooted Charlie") robbed two bank messengers outside the Banque de France in Troyes. Émile fired at one messenger, wounding him in the thigh, and then, to the surprise of Bigfooted Charlie, began to fire at random down the street and into the bank.

He was arrested a month later. French justice was slow, and in 1940, at the time of the invasion, he was still awaiting trial in Troyes Prison. He escaped. In early 1941, he robbed the Credit Lyonnais bank in Rue Notre Dame des Victoires, Paris, killing two bank messengers in cold blood.

Shortly after this he was caught by the Gestapo carrying arms and sent to a military prison; he was then sentenced for the Troyes hold-up in 1937. He escaped by simulating lunacy until he was transferred to the asylum. In 1947, with four associates, he robbed a café in the Rue Lesueur (site of Petiot's crimes) and later executed one of his associates who kept back a brooch. This gave him such a terrible reputation in the underworld that he was not betrayed by professional informers in the usual way, and stayed at liberty a great deal longer than he might otherwise have done.

Over the next few years he took part in many hold-ups, always using sten-guns and Citröen "tractions". After the war, Paris had become a great deal more dangerous than Chicago in the Prohibition era, and gang killings were commonplace. Finally, the police were armed with sub-machine guns, but after accidentally shooting up an old gentleman who was drunk and a bus full of passengers, they were forced by public opinion to be a little more cautious. Finally, a special bandit squad was formed, adequately financed, and run by Charles Chenevier of the Sûreté, who had arrested Buisson in 1937. There was one unsuccessful attempt to arrest Buisson, when a whole convoy of heavily armed police cars rushed out of Paris towards a hotel at Arpajon; but their spectacular exit from Paris excited attention, and someone phoned Buisson, who escaped. However, he was finally arrested in 1955; and tried for the murder of the gangster whom he had "executed". He was guillotined in 1956.

His brother, Jean-Baptiste, nicknamed "Fatalitas" because of his fatalism, shot a restaurant proprietor, Jean Cardeur, when the latter cast aspersions on his dead brother's memory. Maître Carboni, who defended him, turned to the jury as they filed out and said pathetically: "Do not let me have two heads from the same family on my conscience for the rest of my life." (He had defended Émile.) The appeal was successful; Jean-Baptiste was found guilty with a recommendation to mercy, and sentenced to a life sentence of hard labour in Melun Prison.

Jacques Mesrine: "Public Enemy Number One"

At the time of Buisson's execution, a young Frenchman named Jacques Mesrine was already contemplating a career of crime that was to make him for a while the most famous criminal in Europe. Like so many of his larcenous predecessors, Mesrine liked to think of crime as a way of achieving the fame he deserved, and he revelled in his reputation as a modern Robin Hood.

Gangsters

Mesrine was born in Clichy, Paris, in 1937. In 1940, his mother moved her family to Château-Merle, near Poitiers, where she had been brought up, while her husband was in the army. Mesrine was an attractive child, and his biographer Carey Schofield reports that he was usually able to get what he wanted from adults by smiling at them. But he was also solitary. Once, when asked to go and play with other children, he replied; "No, I always have a nicer time on my own."

After the war, the Mesrines returned to Clichy. Mesrine later claimed that he never had enough affection from his father, who worked hard in a textile designing business. He was a poor student at school, but made a strong impression on his schoolmates with his charm, his prowess at fighting, and his love of argument. His constant absenteeism led to his expulsion from two schools. He began joining other teenagers stealing cars for joyrides. At the age of eighteen, he married a beautiful black girl from Martinique, and they moved into a small flat. But he soon found marriage boring and when his wife had a baby, decided that his mother could bring it up.

At nineteen, Mesrine was conscripted into the army, and asked to be sent to Algeria, where the French were trying to put down a Muslim revolt. There was much brutality on both sides. Mesrine thoroughly enjoyed being in action, and received the Military Cross for valour. While in the army, he was divorced from his wife.

His return to civilian life was an anticlimax. He soon committed his first burglary. With two other men, he broke into the flat of a wealthy financier. When a drill broke off in the lock of the safe, he went out to a hardware shop, broke in and got more drills. They escaped with twenty-five million francs.

When de Gaulle came to power in 1958, he began seeking a political solution to the Algerian problem. Mesrine, like many Frenchmen, regarded this as a betrayal. The right-wing General

Salan set up a secret organization, the Organisation Armée Secrète. Mesrine became involved, and it reinforced Mesrine's attitude to law and order — the typical criminal attitude that it is a question of individual choice and that men who can think for themselves should make up their own minds whether to obey the law.

In the spring of 1962, Mesrine was arrested when on his way to rob a bank, and sentenced to three years in prison. He was released on parole a year later. For a while he decided to "go straight". He married a second time, had a young daughter, and now with his father's help, began to study to become an architect. There is evidence that he was a good architect. But when, in late 1964, he was made redundant, he went back to crime. His cool nerve served him remarkably well. Once, in the course of holding up a jewellery shop, the police arrived. Mesrine ran into the back yard, unlatched the gate to make it look as if he had run through, then hid in a dustbin until the coast was clear. On another occasion, he escaped from a flat he was burgling through a lavatory window, and escaped across the roof-tops, walking out of a building further down the street, and asking the police what all the commotion was about.

In 1967 another attempt to "go straight" as an innkeeper — financed by his father — again proved to be a failure as he found respectability too unexciting. He went off with a woman, Jeanne Schneider, and together they carried out a daring robbery at a hotel in Switzerland. In 1968, as one of the most wanted robbers in France, he decided to move to Canada.

He and Schneider went to work for a Montreal million-aire, Georges Deslauriers, as chauffeur and housekeeper, but the gardener took a dislike to Jeanne, and Deslauriers dismissed them. Mesrine's response was to kidnap Deslauriers, and hold him for a $200,000 ransom. Deslauriers managed to escape before the ransom was paid, and Mesrine and Schneider moved to a small town, Percé, where they made the acquaintance of a wealthy widow called Evelyne le Bouthillier. After an evening spent with the pair, Mme le Bouthillier was found strangled. Mesrine always claimed that he knew nothing about the murder.

They slipped over the border into the United States, but were arrested by a border patrol and taken back to Canada. There they were charged with the murder of Mme le Bouthillier. Mesrine was furious at being accused of the murder of an old woman. He claimed that he *had* committed several murders, and tortured people who had insulted him, but that he would have been incapable of this particular crime. Held in the Percé prison pending trial, Mesrine succeeded in escaping by attacking a guard and stealing his keys. He also released Jeanne. They were recaptured only two miles away. Mesrine was given ten years for the kidnapping of Georges Deslauriers; Schneider was given five. But they were acquitted of the murder of Evelyne le Bouthillier.

A year later, Mesrine led a number of other prisoners in a spectacular escape from the "escape-proof" prison of St Vincent de Paul at Laval. He became a celebrity in Canada and it gave him the idea of a still more daring exploit. After robbing a bank in Montreal, he and another escaped convict drove back to the St Vincent de Paul prison with the intention of freeing the remaining prisoners in the top security wing. But when a police car approached them on the way to the prison, Mesrine opened fire. With bullets whistling past them, they escaped back to Montreal. A week later, Mesrine and two accomplices were in the forests near Montreal where they were stopped by two forest rangers. One of the rangers recognized Mesrine, and made the mistake of showing it. Both were shot down, and their bodies dumped in a nearby ditch and covered with branches.

There were more bank robberies – on one occasion, Mesrine robbed the same bank twice because a cashier had scowled at him as he walked out after the first robbery. Then Mesrine met a beautiful nineteen-year-old, Jocelyne Deraiche, who became his mistress. With two accomplices, they crossed the border again into the United States, continuing south to Venezuela where they were able to live comfortably on the profits of their bank robberies, aided by ex-OAS men living there. When a police official told them that Interpol was on their trail, Mesrine and Deraiche flew to Madrid.

All the publicity he had received in Canada had given Mesrine a taste for fame. He decided to become the best known criminal in the world. In the remaining seven years of his life, he achieved that ambition.

Back in France, in 1973 Mesrine committed a dozen armed robberies, netting millions of francs. He gathered around him a gang he could trust. As the hunt for him intensified, he made preparations for the future by examining the courthouse at Compiègne. The precaution proved useful. When police finally caught up with him on 8 March, Mesrine staged a spectacular escape from the Palais de Justice in Compiègne, getting hold of a gun that an accomplice had left in a lavatory, then holding up the court, and escaping with the judge as a human shield. He was shot in the arm in the course of his escape, but had the bullet removed when he was safe in a hideout.

Once again at his old occupation of robbing banks and factories, he carefully nurtured the image of the gentleman crook, the modern Robin Hood. When a female bank clerk accidentally pushed the alarm button, Mesrine commented courteously, "Don't worry, I like to work to music," and went on collecting the money. When he heard his father was dying of cancer in hospital, he made a daring visit to see him dressed as a doctor in a white coat with a stethoscope round his neck. Not long after this, a bank robbery went wrong, and the accomplice waiting in the getaway car was arrested. As a result, the police tracked down Mesrine to his flat in the rue Vergniaud and placed him under arrest.

La Santé prison proved to be escape-proof, and Mesrine passed the time by writing a book, *L'Instinct de Mort* (*The Killer Instinct*), which was smuggled out and appeared in February 1977. In it Mesrine admitted that a previous claim to have killed thirty-nine people was a lie, but it contained detailed descriptions of other murders – for none of which a body had been found. After three and a half years, the prosecution finally opened in May 1977. Mesrine astounded the court by telling his audience that it was easy enough to buy the keys that could open any pair of handcuffs, then extracted a matchbox from the knot of his tie and within seconds had removed his handcuffs. The gesture brought him the kind of publicity that he had now come to crave. He was nevertheless sentenced to twenty years.

A year later Mesrine staged another of his spectacular escapes. An accomplice named Francois Besse squirted soapy water into the eyes of a guard, and Mesrine, who was in the interview room with his lawyer, grabbed some guns from a ventilation shaft. Two warders were made to undress, and the convicts dressed in their uniforms. They let another prisoner, Carman Rives, out of his cell, and then all three rushed across the prison yard. Mesrine and Besse escaped over the wall with a ladder, but Rives was shot.

The police commissioner, Serge Devos, was placed in charge of the squad whose business was to recapture Mesrine. Mesrine moved to Deauville, a seaside resort in Normandy. He was unable to resist the temptation of walking into the local police station, announcing that he was a police inspector from the Gaming Squad, and asking to see the duty inspector. They were told he was not there. As they walked out, one of the policemen said, "That's Mesrine," and the other told him that was impossible. Mesrine then robbed a casino in Deauville, and in the desperate chase that followed, was almost caught. After this, he invaded the home of a bank employee who had given evidence against him at his trial, and forced him to go to the bank and hand over nearly half a million francs.

A Paris department store was the scene of another one of Mesrine's typically quixotic gestures in the summer of 1978. He saw the floor-walker seizing a shoplifter — a boy of fifteen. Mesrine announced himself as a police inspector with special responsibility for juvenile affairs, flashing a fake identity card, then grabbed the boy by the scruff of the neck and led him out of the store. There he let him go. In August, he gave an interview to a journalist from *Paris Match*, which caused a sensation. Then Mesrine came to London where he spent several weeks undisturbed by police. There he planned another astonishing crime — to kidnap the judge who had sentenced him to twenty years in prison. On 10 November 1978 Mesrine and an accomplice returned to France, went to the judge's flat and held up his wife, daughter and son-in-law. But the accomplice was inexperienced, and the daughter succeeded in getting word to the judge's son when he came to the door. Mesrine saw the arrival of the police, ran down the stairs, and as he came face to face with several policemen, pointed behind him. "Quick, Mesrine's up there." And they went rushing past. A young policeman who recognized Mesrine outside was handcuffed to a drainpipe.

In hiding, Mesrine wrote an open letter to the French police denouncing conditions in French prisons and claiming that this had "evoked a fanatical passion for human rights". During his last year there was an obvious deterioration in Mesrine's character. "Mesrine believed in his lies more than anyone else did," said his biographer. "Any suggestion, even from his closest friends, that perhaps he was exaggerating a little, could send him into an uncontrollable fury. He had always been subject to fits of rage, and these were becoming more and more frequent . . . He would smash everything that was in his way, and it is

extraordinary that he never killed anyone while in a rage."
Mesrine explained to journalists — whom he still allowed to
interview him — that he now "identified ideologically with
the extreme left".

When the police finally located his hideout, in a flat in the
rue Belliard, they decided to take no chances. Mesrine had
sworn never to be taken alive. On 2 November 1979
Mesrine came out of the building with his girlfriend, Sylvie
Jean-Jacquot, and walked towards his BMW, parked nearby.
At a road junction, a blue lorry signalled that he wanted to
cut across him and turn right. Mesrine waved him on. The
lorry stopped in front of the car, and another lorry drew up
behind. Four policemen climbed out, and within seconds,
twenty-one bullets had shattered the windscreen. Mesrine
was killed immediately. Sylvie Jean-Jacquot was shot in the
arm, and her dog was also hit. The police flung their arms
around one another and danced for joy.

Chapter Nine

THE KRAYS

Charles Kray was a small, dapper man with sharp black shoes, gleaming black hair and an easy smile. A dealer in second-hand clothes and scrap precious metals, from Hoxton, East London, he came from a family of wanderers, and in the 1930s was happy to travel hundreds of miles to buy stock, knocking on doors and "pestering" people. Charles Kray was considered one of the finest "pesterers" in the business and his neighbours said that the Krays had gypsy blood and were descended from horse-dealers who had settled in this poorest part of London; a drab, depressed area, famous for its pubs and thieves. Here Charles's earnings — twenty or thirty pounds at least most weeks — were riches indeed.

At the age of twenty-four, he married Violet Lee, a seventeen-year-old blonde with blue eyes, whom he met in a dance hall in Hackney. One of three attractive sisters from Bethnal Green in the East End, Violet was a headstrong and romantic girl who had effectively eloped with Charles. When she found out a little more about him, she was content to make do. A good wife, quiet and resourceful, she tolerated his gambling and drinking and their relationship was as equable as these things came. Her own father was a celebrated street-fighter and alcoholic who ruled his family with Victorian severity, and she was grateful to escape.

They lived with Charles's parents over a shop in Stene Street, Hoxton, and Violet was soon pregnant. The doctors told her that she should expect twins. In the event, she gave birth to a single child, who was named Charles David. Three years later she was pregnant again.

Gangsters

, On the night of 17 October 1934, Violet gave birth at home to male twins who arrived within an hour of each other; she called the first Reginald, and the second Ronald.

Violet adored her twins. Their older brother was a placid, easygoing child, but the twins were a demanding pair, and brought out their mother's protective pride. Assailed by the grinding poverty of the time, dreadful housing, disease, malnutrition and inevitable male drunkenness, East End working-class families were more often than not held together by the canniness and sheer persistence of their women, and Violet was to make an exacting matriarch.

Violet dressed her beloved twins in identical clothes. They were pretty babies, swathed in their white angora woolly hats and coats, and everybody clucked over them. They were unusually healthy children for those times, but at the age of three they contracted diphtheria. They were hospitalized – the first time they had been separated from their mother – and Ronald did not make a particularly good recovery. Afterwards, his mother began to worry about him and pay rather more attention to him than to his brother. Young children can be adversely affected by an early dose of diphtheria, so it was perhaps no coincidence that Ronnie was quieter and slower than Reginald; he also began to display a tendency to sulk, and as a toddler made quite violent demands on his mother's affections. The brothers vied for her attention, and watched each other closely, determined that neither should receive more love than the other.

As the pair grew up, they became a strange beast with two heads and four fists, always allied against the world, but often fighting savagely between themselves (though ten minutes later it would all be forgotten). From an early age they fought all-comers. They were surprisingly vicious, and happily took on older boys. Ronnie was the more overtly aggressive. He may have looked for opportunities to denigrate Reggie in his mother's eyes, but he knew he could count on him in a scrap.

Much to Violet's delight, the family moved back to
Bethnal Green, her old neighbourhood. They took a house
in Vallance Road, where they were surrounded by members
of Violet's close family. The area possessed its own
morality, its private code of honour, and a long tradition
of villainy. For those involved in the incessant pub fights,
street brawls and stabbings, it was a violent world. But so
long as the "decent" folk were left alone, the police were
inclined to turn a blind eye.

During the Second World War the Krays' father went
into hiding to evade the call-up; many others in the area
did the same, so much so that the street gained the name
of "Deserter's Corner". The twins became adept at lying to
the police when they came looking for their father. There
were few men around. Ronnie and Reggie spent long
hours in the company of Violet's now reformed and
teetotal father, who regaled them with the folklore of
local fighters and thieves. Violet's sister, Auntie Rose, who
lived round the corner, became a favourite of the twins.
She was a tough, street-fighting woman herself, and from
the beginning she lacked Violet's sentimental illusions
about the twins. She loved them, but she knew and prized
their darker nature and spoiled them rotten. "You're a born
devil," she said to Ronnie. "You know what those eye-
brows of yours mean, meeting in the middle like that? That
you're born to hang . . ."

Violet aspired to respectability and decency; the twins
were imbued with these virtues. This entailed proper
behaviour in public, and the local schoolteacher and vicar
were hard pressed to find fault with Reggie and Ronnie.
They were polite, helpful, punctilious and respectful to their
elders. But increasingly they had other, distinctly violent,
aspirations. They formed juvenile gangs and fought extended campaigns across the Bethnal Green wastelands.
Their elusive father introduced them to old-time cockney
villains, like Dodger Mullins, the "old guvnor" who taught

Boxing twins vow not to fight each other

them the code of the East End criminal. Toughness, pride in one's fighting name, contempt for women and their family values, a willingness to go to the limits in a fight and an utter disregard for the law; the eleventh commandment in Bethnal Green was "thou shalt not grass on thy neighbour".

Aged ten, the Kray twins began to box. Their first fight was in a fairground ring, against each other, and they fought with furious intensity. The bout was declared a draw, with Ronnie taking a black eye and Reggie sporting a bleeding nose. Not only did the fight indicate their prowess at a traditional East End skill, but it also gave the pair an unforgettable taste of notoriety. They were quickly snapped up by a local trainer, and a year later were again fighting each other in the Hackney Schoolboys Final. Reggie won on points, but the violence of the contest frightened the spectators, and Violet made them promise that they would never fight each other again.

Until the age of sixteen, when they turned professional, the twins never lost a bout. Ronnie was tough, but Reggie was canny, and was clearly the one to place the money on, if one was sufficiently familiar with the pair to be able to tell them apart. The twins received a lot of publicity, which fed their appetite for power. At sixteen, they were dominant in the local gang fights. Their commitment to violent force was outstanding: their opponents' serious injuries were caused not only by fists and boots, but by coshes, bicycle chains and broken bottles, which the twins were quick to employ. Ronnie had perfected the technique of cutting an enemy in the face, for which purpose he preferred to use a large sheath knife rather than the traditional razor. The twins bought their first gun, a revolver, and hid it under the floorboards in Vallance Road.

One of their victims, a sixteen-year-old named Harvey, nearly died. There were witnesses, and the twins were remanded in custody. But, by the time the case came to trial, the witnesses, reputedly subjected to veiled threats, were unwilling to testify, and the twins walked free.

Already, Ronnie was getting out of hand. His father had felt his fist, and had become wary of him. He had once had hopes for the twins' future as professional boxers, but he now avoided the increasingly undisciplined pair. Then Ronnie slugged a policeman. Reggie hated the thought of his brother sitting alone in the cells and, acting on the perverse sense of loyalty that was to characterize their relationship, went out and hit the same constable, successfully joining his brother down the local nick. They got off on probation, but Ronnie's reputation as a loose cannon effectively put paid to his professional boxing aspirations. Indeed, despite the good impression these well-mannered boys continued to make on naïve figures of authority, the only people who really exerted any control over them were their Auntie Rose and their beloved, precious and all-forgiving mother, Violet.

In 1952, the twins were called up for National Service in the Royal Fusiliers. Their behaviour on their first day set the tone of their relationship with the Army. They were still being shown around the barracks by a corporal when they announced they didn't care for the environment and were off home. When the corporal tried to stop them, he was hit.

Over the next two years they proceeded to make a mockery of the machinery of army discipline. They were constantly in the guardroom, in military prisons or on the run. They were unafraid of punishment; spartan conditions were merely a trial of their manhood, and their insolent fortitude and skill of fist ensured that all attempts to re-shape them were soon abandoned.

There was something increasingly self-conscious and contrived about the way they presented themselves to the world, dressed in smart blue suits, their tight politeness and control giving way to sudden bouts of orchestrated violence. Their experience of the army sharpened this double act. When, as frequently happened, they were charged with assaulting an officer, it was customary for both to plead ignorance. The authorities found it impossible to ascertain which of these identical, stony-faced young men had actually thrown the punch. Later, towards the end of their relationship with the army, they were incarcerated in the guardroom at Howe Barracks, Canterbury, where they wreaked havoc. Ronnie amused himself by pretending to be "barmy", throwing wild tantrums; Reggie handcuffed the guards; they both burned their bedding and together roundly humiliated a succession of hardened soldiers set on subduing them.

Those with wisdom saw that the best way to treat the twins was with weary forbearance, and looked forward to the day when they could be shot of them. The only man who exerted any significant control was a long-serving, aristocratic adjutant, a languid ex-public schoolboy who had been a prisoner of the Japanese. He appeared untroubled — even bored — by their antics and thus earned their respect. They could be sentimental about a proper gentleman.

Ronnie and Reggie had by now decided that what they wanted was a piece of the "good life". Though not yet certain as to what this was, they nevertheless knew that it wasn't going to come by legitimate means but through the exercise of power in the criminal world. Ronnie was an aficionado of gangster literature and movies; he idolized the organized criminals of Chicago, like Capone, who behaved like emperors.

Military prisons enabled Ronnie and Reggie to meet a whole generation of the criminal fraternity from all over the country. They were to remain excellent networkers. Among the more local of the new friends was Dickie Morgan, a villain from a family of villains. While on the run with him they stayed at his family house in Clinton Road in the East End, a regular thieves' kitchen, where the

Gangsters

Krays were able to mingle with a host of habitual petty criminals. While hiding from the army they also hung around the less salubrious areas of Soho, and made a useful impression on its underworld. Though they were barely nineteen, the twins appreciated that it was in the underworld of the West End, with its gambling clubs, strip joints and drinking holes, that easy money was to be made. If they were to be more than minor criminals from Bethnal Green they need a reputation out West. Out East they would give occasional, breath-taking displays of bar-room fighting. People remembered them, and began to talk about the strange atmosphere that hung around them: an impressive odour of evil.

One Christmas Eve, when the twins were on one of their spells of unauthorized leave from the Army, a policeman named Fisher (who had arrested and returned them to the army once before) came across them sipping a cup of tea in a cafe in Mile End. He invited them to accompany him to the station. They agreed and, once outside, promptly slugged him and ran off. On their capture they were tried for assaulting a policeman, and were sent to Wormwood Scrubs for a month. It made a refreshing change from military prison. Inside, they found themselves accorded a degree of respect generally reserved for important villains. They appreciated the photographs of themselves that appeared in local papers during their trial, sticking the cuttings in their personal scrap-books as evidence of their growing notoriety.

The army finally court-marshalled and ignominiously dismissed the twins. Back in the East End, they began looking for a locus for their career as professional criminals, and fixed upon the Regal, a dilapidated billiard hall in Mile End. A haunt of local gangs who would come, boozed up, to fight and extort, the place was already in trouble. When Reggie and Ronnie started hanging out there, the violence inexplicably increased to such a level that when the twins offered the owners five pounds a week for the tenancy it was gratefully accepted.

The twins made an unexpected success of the place. The violence stopped abruptly, and the hall was efficiently managed and maintained. It remained open day and night, and the twins began to enjoy a heathly income from the billiard tables. They themselves were the main

The Regal gave them a stage on which to parade their theatrical personas. Ronnie was to the fore in this, playing the Chicago mobster, sitting impassively in a chair clad in dark, double breasted suit, small knotted tie and heavy jewellery, occasionally summoning a henchman for a quiet word. He ensured the lights were low, and demanded that the atmosphere be smoky and conspiratorial, as in the movies. He would hand out packets of cigarettes and urge people to gasp away until the room was choked with a fug. He had a liking for the weird and freakish, and would drag in a circus giant or a pair of dwarves to amuse his entourage.

He also liked young boys. Initially, there was an air of philanthropy about his interest in lads culled from the streets. Sometimes he would justify his relationships by pointing out that the kids were also part of a network of informants. But, though he always despised effeminacy, Ronnie was homosexual. It was shortly common knowledge. Later he would bed lads from the area and then give them five pounds to take their girlfriends out for the night, provided they told him which experience they had preferred.

attraction. Their friends began to drop in regularly and hang around just to see what might happen: life was never dull. There might be a fight on the premises, as when the Maltese gang called in, looking for protection money, and were cut to ribbons with cutlasses; or the twins might form up a raiding party and drop in on a neighbouring pub for a brawl. Watching them punch, kick, slice and stab, their friends were consistently struck by the intent and serious nature of Kray violence. Despite the twins' small stature, they were never to come off worse in a fight. They developed specialities. Reggie perfected a trick he called his "cigarette punch", for which he would sucker the prospective target by offering him a cigarette with his right hand. When the man opened his jaw to put the cigarette in his mouth, Reggie would catch him with a left hook. An open jaw shatters very easily and the "cigarette punch" floored many. Ronnie preferred to cut people, though he considered the razor an inadequate weapon, and preferred a knife or sharpened cutlass. He also fantasized about using guns, of which he had an expanding collection. It was undoubtedly Ronnie who was the more frightening of the pair.

At first there was little organized purpose to the twins' violent forays. But the loose groupings of admirers and minor criminals soon began to form into a distinct gang. Ronnie had found new role models in Lawrence of Arabia and other military heroes. He began to organize, and instil obedience into, the evolving gang. He learned the value of intelligence and propaganda, and began to plan raids in detail, evolving complex tactics. One day somebody christened him "the Colonel". The nickname stuck.

The Krays were often seen as one personality split between two identical bodies, and in this collective psychology it was the violent aspect of Ronnie that was in the ascendant. The aspect of reason, and a modicum of self-

The money didn't make Ronnie happy.
Increasingly, he wanted to kill somebody. He
fantasized about it, drawing up lists of those
who merited death, and cutting the ends of his
unused bullets to make them into dum-dums
capable of blowing a man to pieces. When a
local car-dealer got into a spot of bother with a
client and asked for help, Ronnie went after him
with a Luger and shot the man in the leg, just as
he was apologizing to the dealer for his rash
behaviour. Reggie had once again to do the
tidying up. He bought time by letting himself be
arrested in Ronnie's place. By the time he got
round to telling the police that they had
arrested Reginald, not Ronald, Kray, his brother
was safely hidden away, and the victim and all
witnesses were suffering from amnesia. Reggie
was not best pleased with Ronnie, who
retaliated by telling him that he was an amateur
who'd never have the balls to kill a man.

restraint, represented by Reggie, was gradually being
suppressed.

For the moment, the gang – which would one day
become known throughout London as "the Firm" – served
as a form of publicity for the Krays. Their aura of control
made the Regal into a safe house and meeting place for
criminals, who could make contacts, exchange information
and conceal their stolen goods. The twins took a cut from
the crimes they helped arrange; Reggie generally nego-
tiated. They began to pull complicated con-tricks, and
extort regular protection money from pubs, illicit gambling
dens and bookmakers.

Gangsters

As their activities took shape, they presented a challenge to some of the established local gangs. Three dockers, all brothers, who unofficially ran Mile End and Poplar, issued a challenge. They were big men – much bigger than the Krays – and all good amateur boxers. To the disappointment of their followers, the Krays refused to talk about the affair. As the appointed date – a Sunday morning – approached, many began to think that the twins were opting for discretion rather than valour. Ronnie and Reggie seemed wholly unconcerned. They spent the Saturday night as usual, getting thoroughly drunk (their capacity for alcohol was stupendous), and lounged around the Regal quietly on the Sunday morning, sipping tea and chatting amiably. Then, with a nod to each other, they strolled down the road to the pub where, in an empty bar, the dockers were waiting. By the time the manager of the pub thought the twins must have had a good hiding and went back into the bar, it looked like an abattoir. Two of the dockers were laid out and Ronnie was carving some finishing touches on the third.

The twins looked forward to the day when they would assume control of London's gangland. Nor were they content to take it in the discreet way in which these matters were customarily handled. None of the old criminals would start a gang-war if it could be avoided. Not so Reggie and Ronnie. They longed for confrontation; they were convinced of their invulnerability, and in the face of this boundless confidence, most of their opponents simply melted away.

They allied themselves with an old villain, Jack Spot, who with another, Billy Hill, ruled the town, and constantly tried to precipitate an all-out struggle for power in the Chicago style. Armed to the teeth with guns, they prowled the streets in their car, looking for trouble. Finally, Ronnie got a chance to shoot a gun. Spot and Hill had both retired and there were new Italian gangs moving in on the West End.

The twins believed they were on a hit-list of potential opponents. Ronnie took his favourite Mauser, drove to the Italians' pub and discharged three shots. Fortunately, despite his passion for guns, he was a notoriously bad shot, and missed everybody.

The "Firm" grew. By 1955 there was a buzz of money around the twins. Funded by an ever-growing protection racket, they looked like they might be on their way to wealth and now drove big American cars. Their henchmen did well too. Each could expect some forty pounds a week as their share of the proceeds from extortion, and both Reggie and Ronnie were lavish with the cash: they enhanced their charitable reputation by looking after the families of those doing a stint in prison and were always approachable for a hardship loan.

Then, on 5 November 1956, Ronald Kray was sentenced to prison for three years. He had been convicted of inflicting grievous bodily harm on a young man named Terry Martin, a member of a gang from neighbouring Watney Street. Martin's gang had beaten up an ex-boxer named Joe Ramsey. Ramsey was important to the Krays: he had just secured them their first toe-hold in the West End as his partners in The Stragglers, a shabby drinking club. Martin was the only member of the gang the twins could get their hands on. They held him while Ramsey sliced him up with a bayonet, and then put the boot in. Martin nearly died. Reggie went home. Ronnie, still attired in blood-stained clothing and armed to the teeth, was stopped by the police, as he drove frantically around the area, looking for more trouble. Ronnie went to Wandsworth gaol, where he seemed quite happy. He was respected by both prisoners and staff, and lacked for nothing. With help from outside, he soon had the traditional prison trade in tobacco under his thumb, ate well and did no work.

With the erratic Ronnie safely under lock and key, Reggie began to prosper. He missed Ronnie, but at last

Ronnie liked to have the local barber come over to his house and shave him in the morning, something he had read that Chicago gangsters did. The tailor also had to call personally, and he had his shirts and suits delivered to the door. He took up riding and spent the weekends playing the country squire in a Suffolk village. He had a pet Doberman, which he adored. But he remained contemptuous of the moderate policies of Reggie and Charlie and wanted an immediate return to the old days of violence and petty extortion. He upset people, careering drunkenly around the East End, demanding protection money from clubs in which the Krays already had a stake and publicly insulting the Italian gangs with whom Reggie had carefully forged peace. He accused Reggie of having gone soft, which he blamed on his brother's taste for women.

it was not necessary to sacrifice business interests for the sake of theatrical violence. Reggie opened a club, The Double R (after Ronnie and himself) on the Bow Road. He had always felt that the East End lacked a decently run club with a bit of glamour. The club was respectable, and had good singers and a lively atmosphere. Its association with two men popularly believed to be violent criminals also gave it a sheen of fashionable, sexy violence. One or two playboys and pop-stars began to roll in, looking for something to stimulate their jaded palates. The legitimate world and criminal world, high life and low life, the overtly proper and the covertly perverse mingled freely at the Double R.

Charlie Kray, the twins' brother, began to work along-side Reggie. They opened another club in the East End, and then started a gambling den next to Bow Police Station. Later they formed a friendship with their former enemy, the retired gangster Billy Hill. Hill had interests in illicit gambling throughout the West End that he still needed to have minded, and gave Charlie and Reggie a stake in the lucrative business. With Parliament on the verge of legalizing gambling, the Krays realized that they could soon quit the East End and be wealthy and powerful on a grand scale, without having to resort to Ronnie's style of violence. Ronnie could be thoroughly misogynistic; free from his influence, Reggie began to enjoy the company of women. He had nights out in the West End and moved in society. He looked happy.

Ronnie was not having an enjoyable time. His good behaviour had secured his transfer to a prison on the Isle of Wight. It was easygoing, but Ronnie was lost without the familiar criminal company and respect he had been accorded in Wandsworth. He grew depressed, and then paranoid. He thought that people believed he was an informer; then he saw the outlines of a conspiracy and imagined that he was under constant surveillance by people who wanted to torture him. He retreated into himself and spent days sitting in the corner of his cell. He finally broke and, after a bout of terrifying violence, was put in a straitjacket. Then his beloved Auntie Rose died of leukaemia. Ronnie slid into madness, and shortly after Christmas 1957 was certified insane.

He was diagnosed as paranoid schizophrenic. Transferred to a Surrey mental institution, he began to make a recovery, assisted by large doses of the drug Stematol. But so long as he was certified insane, there was no prospect of his release.

Under prison regulations, anyone who was certified insane, escaped and stayed at large for longer than six weeks had to be certified again on recapture. If Ronnie could escape, and appear sane on recapture, he would be allowed to complete his original sentence.

In the summer of 1958, Reggie helped his brother to escape, and hid him in the Suffolk countryside. The twins had spent a spell there during the Blitz, and the country seemed to calm Ronnie down. He lived in a caravan deep in woodland, accompanied by a trusted bodyguard who did the cooking and cleaning. Reggie kept him well supplied with boys and alcohol and Ronnie amused himself by getting his bodyguard to play "the hunting game" in which they stalked each other with air-guns. But he was soon bored. He was jealous of Reggie's public prominence and missed London. He implored Reggie to let him make the occasional late-night foray to the Double R. Against the better advice of his brother Charlie, Reggie agreed. Soon Ronnie was dressing up as Reggie and strolling through the streets of Whitechapel.

But each time he returned to the country, Ronnie fell back into his former depression. He brooded, and began to mutter ominously about murder. He was moved from the caravan into a neighbouring farm. After the police called to make a routine check, he lapsed once more into paranoia, accusing Reggie of being an impostor: he was not his brother, but a Russian spy.

Even Reggie was frightened. The family discreetly consulted psychiatrists and doctors, but the drugs prescribed had a limited effect. Ronnie was contained by the consumption of two bottles of gin a day.

After Ronnie attempted suicide, the family realized that he had to be returned to a secure mental hospital; they must surrender him to the authorities. Reggie let the police know that if they came around to Vallance Road they could pick his brother up. Ronnie was unsuspecting, and when the police called, he went without a murmur.

With treatment, he was allowed to finish his prison sentence and was released in the spring of 1959. He immediately suffered a fit of paranoia and, convinced that the Russians were coming to get him, was sedated in a hospital. Again he recovered, but his personality was irrevocably altered. Before his breakdown he had been an unnerving presence. Now he was hysterically excitable, wholly crazed and dangerous, devoid of any vestige of conventional conscience and trapped within his own grotesque fantasies.

As a consequence of one of Ronnie's rash pledges of loyalty, Reggie found himself embroiled in a dispute over money between a shop-owner and a small-time crook. He went to prison for eighteen months. Charlie Kray melted into the background and Ronnie was free to indulge his taste for open warfare, slowly destroying the business they had built up.

Income plummeted. Then, quite coincidentally, something profitable happened. Ronnie fell out with Perac Rachman, later notorious as a landlord specializing in extortion. In order to get Ronnie off his back, Rachman showed him how the Krays could get their hands on Esmerelda's Barn, a Mayfair gambling club, the haunt of stars and minor royalty.

The twins now had a business advisor, Leslie Payne. A canny man, who had just been declared bankrupt and badly needed the work, "Payne the Brain" was a principal factor in the rise of the Krays. Latterly he had managed to exert some control over Ronnie. Reggie was out of prison pending appeal and, together with Payne, the twins called on the owner of Esmerelda's Barn. Acting on information Rachman had given them, Payne made the man an offer. After a glance at Reggie and Ronnie, the man decided not to refuse it. The club did well. Soon the twins were making £40,000 a year each, without having to lift a finger. But Reggie lost his appeal, and went back to prison.

Ronnie carried on playing the role of king gangster. He had money, lavish clothes, expensive cars, a flat in the West

When Reggie got out of prison he was in love
with Frances Shea, the sister of a man the
twins had known since their youth. She was
sixteen, eleven years younger than Reggie. In
prison he had written to her every day. He
dreamed of a perfect marriage; with his fairy-
tale bride he would at last lead the good life,
free of the strain of crime, and free of Ronnie.
His twin knew Frances was a threat. He hated
her. At first, Reggie's society contacts and
wealth impressed Frances and her parents.
When he first proposed to her, in the autumn
of 1961, she turned him down, on the grounds
that she was too young. He persisted; he was
possessive but also charming and generous,
and courted her assiduously over the next
four years. She married him on 20 April 1965,
at St James, Bethnal Green. It was the East
End wedding of the year. David Bailey
photographed the wedding and the church was
packed with journalists and voyeurs from the
world of show business. Within eight weeks
Frances, at last party to the truth about
Reggie's life, could take no more. She fled
back to her parents. Reggie could not leave
her alone. She became frightened and
withdrawn. She had a breakdown and tried to
kill herself a number of times. She tried to
get a divorce, but then agreed to attempt a
reconciliation with Reggie, who claimed he
was a changed man. On 6 June 1967 they
booked air-tickets for a second honeymoon.
That night, Reggie dreamed she had taken her

life and, as dawn broke, went around to her
parents where she was staying. It was true.
She apparently died a virgin.

End and all the pretty boys he could manage; for a while he
fell in love, and paraded his boy about as if he were a young
mistress, tenderly calling him "son" and referring to himself
as "your old Dad". But at heart he remained an unhappy
and sick man. He despised the wealthy, confident clientele
of the club. They made him feel insecure. He wanted an
entourage of people he could control and began to attract a
seedier variety of customer, offering hard-up nobility and
habitual losers unlimited credit. Though the club's profits
fell, it remained a gold-mine, and its respectability was
ensured for a time when they persuaded Lord Effingham –
the first of a string of tame peers – to join the board of
management. Charlie urged his brothers to invest their
wealth quickly in clubs and betting shops, but Ronnie
resisted. He knew that if the Krays became legitimate, he
would cease to be of any significance.

While Ronnie now believed himself to be a reincarnation
of Attilla the Hun and a Samurai warrior, read "Mein
Kampf" and planned to create an army that would take
the world by force, Reggie kept the business going and
efficiently muscled into the protection rackets of the West
End. He also established fruitful contacts with foreign
organizations looking for a piece of the action in London
and, aided by the ingenuity of Payne, the twins were able to
execute a string of lucrative frauds. They began to expand
outside London, taking over clubs in Birmingham and
Leicester. They cultivated a reputation for philanthropy,
giving generously to charity; they were not shy of publicity, and their faces were soon appearing regularly in
national newspapers. They granted interviews to eminent

Ronnie met Ernest Shinwell, son of the Labour politician, who interested him in a plan to build a new township costing several million pounds in the bush outside an obscure Nigerian town. Ronnie became obsessed with the plan, certain that it would guarantee immortality, and visited the country as a VIP guest of the Nigerian government. When the grandiose design collapsed, he was bitterly upset. An old confederate of the twins had the misfortune to catch Ronnie on a night after he had received the bad news. He touched Ronnie for five pounds and made a cheerful jibe about his weight. Ronnie took him into the bathroom and cut most of his face off. It took seventy stitches to put him back together again.

journalists, and Ronnie approached one to ghost his autobiography, but the offer was declined.

In 1963, they made their first important political contact: Joan Littlewood, the legendary theatre director, introduced them to the influential and corrupt Tom Driberg, then Labour MP for Barking. A future Chairman of the Labour party, who later became a respected member of the House of Lords, Driberg was one of a number of eminent pederasts whom Ronnie was to form mutually rewarding relationships with. In return for support, Ronnie provided flesh to order. His parties became famous, and he began to receive invitations to stately homes outside London.

In the summer of 1964, the *Sunday Mirror* alleged the existence of a homosexual relationship between a prominent member of the House of Lords and a "leading thug in the London underworld". It also claimed that it had pictures to prove it. Though they were not yet named, it was known that the men referred to were Lord Boothby and Ronald Kray.

The twins were in two minds about the happening. There was no such thing as bad publicity, but homosexuality was illegal, and any investigation into Boothby might lead to their activities. The police had long been looking for something that would give them a hold over the Krays. But when the police realized that a number of politicians might be involved, they backed off. The photographer who had supplied the newspaper with the pictures suddenly wanted them back; Boothby denied everything and received an apology and £40,000 from the newspaper's parent company. Even Ronnie got an apology. The editor of the *Sunday Mirror* got the sack.

The following January, a known associate of the Krays entered a West End club, demanded money for the twins and, when it was not forthcoming, smashed the place up. The police believed that they at last had something on the twins. They were arrested and charged with demanding money with menaces. It is alleged that with Boothby's help, they were able to command the services of the best criminal lawyers in London, and Boothby even had the chutzpah to raise their case sympathetically in the House of Lords. After two trials, and amid whispers that both jurors and witnesses had been subject to unseen pressure, the twins were acquitted. "To some extent I share your triumph" wrote Boothby to Ronald Kray. No doubt he had a considerable share in it. The twins walked free in a blaze of triumphant publicity. Reggie married Frances Shea almost immediately.

This perverse alliance of the Krays and respected establishment forces ensured that henceforth there was a virtual news-blackout on their criminal activities. They seemed unchallengeable, and were left alone to consolidate their hold on London. Over the next four years they re-organized protection rackets on a scale never seen in

Britain, before or since. They dealt freely with the New York Mafia, marketing vast quantities of stolen US bonds, looked after the Mob's interests in London, and swindled and intimidated with absolute impunity.

In March 1966, at Ronnie's instigation, they found themselves in a rather unnecessary war with a lesser gang run by the Richardson brothers, scrap metal merchants from South London. Their interests should never have clashed. Ronnie got hold of a pair of Browning machine-guns, and the twins prepared for the bloody battle the "Colonel" longed for.

On 8 March there was an unrelated shoot-out when the Richardsons tried to steam-roller a local gang at Mr Smith's club in Catford. It left one man dead and another two seriously injured. The Richardsons came off worse, and there was clearly no need for the Krays to take any further action against them: they were finished as rivals.

But Ronnie wanted to have his say in the Richardsons' demise. There was a lesser Richardson member called Cornell, who he knew had once called him a "fat poof". Taking his Mauser 9mm pistol, Ronnie had himself driven to The Blind Beggar, the Richardsons' hang-out. He and his driver walked in; Cornell was sitting at the bar. The driver loosed off a couple of shots to clear the bar. Then, at point-blank range, Ronnie blew Cornell's head to pieces. It was the most satisfying moment of his career.

It would be two years before the police could persuade anyone to talk.

Reggie had to clear up the mess. He put his twin into hiding in an obscure flat in Finchley, where Ronnie was engulfed by another savage depression and bouts of waking nightmares during which he would turn violent or attempt suicide. But Reggie managed to contain him and still keep the business going, though the strain was telling. There was now an air of unnatural self-control about Reggie. Still good-looking, he had become thin and had dark rims under his bloodshot eyes. Ronnie was fat and swollen, his thickened face permanently distorted with anger.

By the spring of 1967, just as Ronnie was calming down, Reggie's wife, Frances, committed suicide. Reggie went off the rails. He drank himself insensible and veered between violent self-reproach and utter hatred for her family who, he said, had turned Frances against him. After the funeral, Reggie became more like his erratic twin. Aside from the hour he spent at Frances's grave each day, talking to her ghost, he was drunk most of the time; with encouragement from Ronnie, he started looking for people he could hurt. The first was a former friend called Frederick, who he believed might have said something derogatory about his dead wife. Fuelled by a violent row with Ronnie, Reggie turned up at Frederick's house and shot him in the leg. He shot and wounded another man at a club in Highbury, then slit open the face of an old boxer with whom he had a vague dispute. One or two of the Firm's members went missing following disagreements with the twins.

Ronnie was still determined that his brother should kill a man in cold blood. The eventual victim was Jack "The Hat" McVitie. A criminal whose nerve had long gone, McVitie was a good-natured man who derived his courage from alcohol and pills. Ronnie heard that Leslie Payne had struck a deal with the police and was grassing on the twins' activities. He offered McVitie £500 to kill Payne. Jack "The Hat" bungled the attempt. Ronnie was furious, and wanted his money back; he issued threats. Reggie briefly smoothed things over. Then McVitie got drunk, and wandered into a club waving a shotgun and saying he was looking for the twins. Word of this reached Ronnie.

On a Saturday in October 1967 Reggie and Ronnie Kray told two of their henchmen to find McVitie and bring him to a party they had arranged in a dingy flat in the East End. The owner of the flat, a blonde girl they knew well, was happy to loan them her premises for the evening. Surprisingly, McVitie, who probably had no recollection of his previous behaviour, came willingly. As he walked in through the door, Reggie shot at him. The gun jammed. McVitie tried to dive through the window, but got stuck. Ronnie pulled him back; Reggie had taken a carving knife from one of the gang. McVitie looked at him in bewilderment; Ronnie insisted; Reggie struck the point of the knife into his head below the eye. As McVitie sank to the floor, Reggie stabbed him repeatedly in the stomach and then impaled him through the throat to the floor. The twins took a holiday in Suffolk. The body was never found.

Detective Chief Inspector "Nipper" Read of Scotland Yard had a long-standing battle with the twins. They considered him highly dangerous and had done all they could to ruin his career. His failure to get them convicted on charges of extortion two years previously had nearly done for him. He was happy to stay away from them, but on being posted to Scotland Yard in 1967 was promptly put in charge of their case. It was an unenviable task. There was very little documentation of their activities. Any possible conviction was wholly dependent on persuading victims and villains to talk and the criminal code of silence had ensured this had not happened.

But Read was convinced that if he could persuade one to talk then many would follow. Leslie Payne had heard about the offer Ronnie had made to McVitie, and was the first to agree. Once he had outlined the Krays' activities in a statement two hundred pages long, Read knew that he had the basis of a case. With exacting slowness, his team began to pick up corroborating statements from reluctant witnesses. Read hoped that once people saw the Krays were under lock and key they would be happier to come forward. In particular, the barmaid at The Blind Beggar, who had witnessed the shooting of Cornell, might at last talk.

It was 9 May 1968 before they felt they had sufficient

evidence to hold the twins. It was a gamble, but they could delay no longer. At 7 a.m., the police smashed in the doors of the house where the twins were staying and dragged them out of their beds. They had been out drinking until 5 a.m.. Ronnie was with his latest boy; Reggie, with a girl from Walthamstow.

With the twins awaiting trial, the police quickly rounded up the members of the already disintegrating Firm. With no Firm, the twins had no way of reaching those who talked and the wall of silence that had protected them collapsed. Their sources of money vanished; their support melted away; they had to apply for legal aid. The barmaid from The Blind Beggar did speak as a witness for the prosecution. Reggie was charged with being an accessory to that killing, and Ronnie as an accessory to the McVitie murder. On 8 March 1969, at the end of the longest and most expensive criminal trial in Britain, Mr Justice Melford Stevenson sentenced them to life imprisonment, and recommended that this should be not less than thirty years each.

They were only thirty-four years old. Apart from attending their mother's funeral, they have remained in prison ever since. Reggie is in Parkhurst on the Isle of Wight. A "Category A" prisoner, his life is spent in solitary confinement. He now suffers from acute depression and is haunted by the past. He hopes that he will still live to re-marry and settle in the country, but there is no parole for Category A prisoners. Ronnie was originally with him in Parkhurst, but was certified insane and transferred to Broadmoor. He lives well, dresses nattily and has become rather keen on art and health food. Although sedated by drugs, he still considers himself the Colonel, and has broad fantasies about his importance. He has plenty of hopes for the future, and no regrets about the past.

Ronnie Kray

Chapter Ten

JACK SPOT AND BILLY HILL: THE LONDON VILLAINS

F or many years before the Kray twins brought their particular brand of American-style organized crime and violence to London, the sprawling, fog-bound city of the 1930s and 1940s was run by two legendary villains: Jack Spot and Billy Hill.

At various times close friends and bitter rivals, both claimed the title of "King of London's Underworld". Although violence was endemic in their circles, it rarely erupted onto the streets or involved the public, and so long as they remained discreet, the police — many of whom formed close relations with the villains — were content to leave the criminals to themselves.

Far better the devil you know, the argument went. Underpaid bobbies on the beat were frequently accused of "rolling" those too drunk to resist, and stealing their possessions. This is the origin of the saying: "If you want to know the time, ask a policeman". Policemen were never without a watch, often donated by an unsuspecting drunk.

Guns, although increasingly available after the First World War, were rarely used and killings were less frequent than they would become under the Krays. The old gangs rarely indulged in the spectacular gun battles that American gangsters were so fond of. Enemies and traitors were not machine-gunned from cars but visited by the "chiv-man", who would carefully slice a face up with his

Gangsters

In the 1920s many major criminals in London
tended to be men renowned for their sheer
masculine toughness rather than as businessmen-
gangsters. East End villains such as Jew Jack
"The Chopper King", Wassle Newman, Jimmy
Spinks and Dodger Mullins (who was later to
become something of a mentor to the Krays)
were legendary for their displays of brute force.
Newman was reputed to toughen his fists by
tossing bricks in the air and punching them as
they came down; but he was no master of
organized crime. He simply enjoyed being a
bully, and would go into pubs and take away the
customers' beer, daring them to protest. Mullins
was notorious for his perfunctory views on the
fairer sex, and once disposed of a girlfriend he
had tired of by pushing her out of a moving car.
She broke her back. Spinks was a bully like
Newman; when actually asked to pay for some
fish and chips he was guzzling, he tossed the cat
belonging to the shop's owners into the chip-
fryer. One Glasgow "hard man", Jimmy "Razzle
Dazzle" Dalziel, was so afraid of having his
masculinity questioned that he would always
dance with a member of his gang, the "Parlour
Boys", rather than be seen being sentimental
with a woman.

taped-down cut-throat razor, or chop through their collar
bones with his little hatchet.

In a fight, gangs used knives, razors, pick-axe handles,
hatchets and the fist and the boot. But, for generations, their

favourite weapon was the beer-bottle. If you carried a gun or a knife, you could be in serious trouble if the police stopped you. But an innocuous beer-bottle was entirely legitimate. Quite apart from providing suitable sustenance before an affray, it made an excellent club. It could quickly be smashed and its broken, jagged edges thrust into the face of an opponent with devastating results. It also made an excellent missile.

The English underworld in the early part of the century provided a number of illegal but nevertheless essential services. It supplied prostitution, gambling and out of hours drinking facilities to the public. The men who ran the illegal rackets were "wide-men"; the them, the respectable, hard-working populace were "mugs", waiting to be fleeced.

During the years of acute poverty, and particularly in the 1930s, prostitution was rampant in London, as women discovered that they could make a comparatively good living on the streets. They could get through twenty or thirty clients in a shift of four hours, and as they charged from ten shillings to a pound a time, the wages of sin were quite decent. Many prostitutes came from abroad. Marthe Watts, a French woman, hated the English climate, but was surprised at the leniency of the police. She was also perturbed by the sexual tastes of the average Englishman. She once said she was astonished at the number of men who wanted her to tie them up and beat them. Those who controlled the prostitution rackets also tended to come from abroad: until 1929, the principal racketeers were a Frenchman, Casimire Micheletti, and a Spanish dancer, Juan Antonio Castanar. When "Mad Emile" Berthier, a known associate of Castanar, mistook a French pimp called Charlie "The Acrobat" for Micheletti and slashed him to death in a seedy Frith Street dive, the police deported the rival pimps. The prostitution racket was taken over by "Red Max" Kessel, a heavily scarred Latvian, whose bullet ridden body turned up in a ditch in Hertfordshire. Another infamous pimp was Eddie Manning, a Jamaican dope dealer. Being black he was viewed, in keeping with the morals of the time, with particular horror, because of the power he exerted over white women. Manning was called the "wickedest man in London". After imprisonment in 1929 he died of a cocaine habit.

In the nineteenth century, betting on racehorses became a national past-time. But it remained illegal to lay a bet anywhere other than at the racecourse. This was to remain the case until the Betting and Gaming Act of 1960. Despite the illegal status of off-course bookmakers, there were well over 15,000 of them practising in the 1920s, and it was estimated that illegal bookmaking had an annual turnover of between £350 and £450 million. The police and the bookmakers had an unofficial arrangement, whereby the police would satisfy the public desire to see an occasional prosecution by periodically rounding up a number of bookmakers. They would be compensated by their fellows for any lost earnings. In return the police could expect to be well treated, receiving regular payments, and the odd case of whisky.

Criminals are almost exclusively attracted to sources of money, and such a vast business naturally invited the attention of protection gangs. These, apart from charging a bookmaker for his "pitch" at the racetrack and taking a substantial percentage of his profits from illegal off-course betting, would protect him against theft and ensure that his debtors paid up. The last was most important. Gambling debts were not enforceable by law, and losses were vast. Between 1918 and 1956, the underworld was largely dominated by the race-gangs. Jack Spot ran one of these.

The son of Polish Jews who had come to England in the 1890s, Jack Spot, who generally gave his real name as Jack Comer, was born in Whitechapel in 1912. It was an industrious, hard working and law-abiding community,

The use of hard drugs such as heroin and cocaine became more common in the 1920s. The "Bright Young Things" of the "Roaring Twenties" were often young women determined to live the bright life and take their chances with death. They were known as "dopers" and lived lives which consisted principally of drugs and parties. Countless "Bright Young Things" began to succumb to drug overdoses. Among these were many aspiring actresses and society hostesses. Billie Carleton, a popular actress much sought after (not only for her acting skill), died of cocaine poisoning after attending the victory celebrations in November 1918. Freda Kempton, who was a hostess at a club run by the legendary "madame" Kate Meyrick, died of an overdose of cocaine in March 1922. The actress Brenda Dean Paul was crippled by her addiction. These – and many other casualties – were laid at the door of "Brilliant" Chang, an immaculately groomed Chinese man, who owned two restaurants in the heart of the West End. He was strongly suspected of being a substantial gangster specializing in the opium trade, and his close liaisons with beautiful young women caused outrage and indignation. As late as the 1950s one national newspaper remembered him as "an arch-fiend, who would stop at nothing to gain his mastery over beautiful women". Chang was arrested in 1924, but only imprisoned for fourteen months. On his release he was deported, but in exile he was still thought to have a substantial interest in the London drugs trade.

Darby Sabini and his brothers Joe, Charles, Harry Boy and Fred came from Saffron Hill, Clerkenwell, the heart of London's Italian community. In the early 1920s they wrested control of the lucrative South of England racecourses from Billy Kimber and his Birmingham gang, with considerable assistance from the Flying Squad (then one of the first mobile police units) with which Darby Sabini had reached an "understanding". For fourteen years Sabini and his brothers maintained a discreet but all-powerful hold over the racing world. Their shootings and stabbings went largely unreported, but the police were quick to swoop on affrays instigated by the vengeful Birmingham mob, or one of the other London race-gangs. Once Sabini was attacked at the Fratalanza Club in Great Bath Street by a rival gang, the four Cortesi brothers, who blazed away at the gangster and his family. It was their first attempted shooting, however, and they missed. The four men were quickly rounded up. But only two of them were found guilty of "attempted murder", and the judge held that this was an internecine dispute, unworthy of public concern: the men only received three years each. In the end Sabini fell from grace as a result of a lost libel case. A newspaper called him "Britain's leading gangster". Sabini sued, and then failed to turn up in court. He lost and was ordered to pay modest costs, which, being a profligate, he couldn't manage, and he had to declare himself bankrupt. The excessive publicity he received perpetually discredited him in the eyes of his fellow criminals.

and from an early age Spot, who was restless and aggressive, stood out. His brothers and sister were employed in tailoring and dressmaking but Spot hung around the local boxing clubs and gyms, where the local ne'er-do-wells would congregate.

He established a reputation as a fearless fighter and, in those days of rising anti-Semitism, he soon found himself inundated with pleas for protection from Jewish bookmakers, businessmen, promoters and shopkeepers who were threatened by the activities of fascists. When Sir Oswald Mosley attempted to march through the East End with his Blackshirts in 1936, Spot and his entourage happily decimated Mosley's bodyguard.

He was increasingly drawn to the lucrative world of the racetracks and the "spielers": the small, illicit gambling clubs that were widespread throughout Soho and the West End. These were the scene of many confrontations between Jewish and Italian gangsters. Though Spot took his fair share of beatings – he was thrashed to the point of death with billiard cues by a mob from Islington – he earned a reputation for his almost foolhardy courage.

By the early 1940s Spot, backed by his ferocious race-gang, was the emerging force in the criminal underworld. Following a police clamp-down on the "spielers" in 1940, Spot and his cronies found themselves dragooned into the army. Spot hated it, objecting to the bad pay, rotten food, harsh discipline and rampant anti-Semitism. He had no compunction about belting his superiors and, after three torrid years, the marine regiment admitted failure and discharged him as mentally unstable.

> Teetotal Spot often had the mickey taken for
> drinking only lemonade. He didn't mind and
> favoured attacking his opponents when the
> alcohol had rendered them incapable of
> retaliation. He liked to attack the opposition in
> West End pub toilets. As he said himself: "I used
> to knock 'em out in the lavatory, that was my
> surgery. I used to follow 'em into the toilet and
> bomp! Leave 'em in the piss."

Spot returned to the Blitz-devastated East End to find
that his parents were dead and his family long dispersed. He
became involved with the spivs, but after an altercation
with a local hard man (in which he nearly succeeded in
killing him with a tea-pot), he fled to Leeds, the black-
market capital of the north, and a haven for deserters,
gamblers and racketeers.

Here his strength, lack of fear and his alcoholic abstinence
quickly gave him an advantage over the local gangsters. He
looked after club-owners and bookies, and after the war
moved back into London's gambling clubs. High wages, the
profits of crime and the recklessness induced by realizing
one was still alive created a vast boom in post-war
gambling.

From a club in St Botolph's row, on the outskirts of the
City, Spot also ran his extensive racetrack business. After a
pitched battle with the Islington mob, which brought him
control of Ascot race-course, his only serious challengers
were the White gang. But the White gang had grown soft,
and met their Waterloo at the Stork club in Sackville Street,
where Spot and his men coshed and "chived" them into
bloody submission.

Spot's gang were also involved in lorry hijacking and big
"project" heists. It was thought that he was behind the

Billy Hill, 1956

Gangsters

Motorized crime and car theft began to boom in
the 1920s. Fast transport and the prospect of a
swift getaway widened the prospective
criminal's catchment area. Two of the most
famous motor bandits were "Ruby" Sparks and
his long-time lover and side-kick the "Bobbed-
Haired Bandit". Ruby earned his nickname while
working as a cat-burglar: he unwittingly stole a
priceless cache of rubies from an Indian prince,
but believing they were fake, gave them all
away. With the "Bobbed-Haired Bandit" he
turned to motorized smash and grab raids. The
first time he tried throwing a brick at a window
it bounced back at him, but he soon developed a
successful technique, though it often meant that
he lacerated his arms. He would hold the gashes
together with bulldog clips until the "Bobbed-
Haired Bandit" sewed him up. The police
admired the "Bobbed-Haired Bandit", a Jewish
girl from a respectable family who had turned to
crime after an unhappy love affair. She drove a
Mercedes and sported a black beret. After five
years she and Ruby were caught, but got off
with light sentences. After Sparks escaped from
a spell in prison in 1940 they teamed up again.
But they were old and tired. She had grey in
her hair and wore spectacles. After a few
abortive raids they finally retired.

abortive 1948 Heathrow airport robbery, when ten men
armed with lead pipes and with nylon stockings over their
heads drove up to the airport in a lorry, coshed the security
guards into submission, and broke into a warehouse which

was reputed to contain ten million pounds in gold ingots. Unfortunately it was a Flying Squad trap, and they were assaulted by a phalanx of psyched-up policemen. After a brutal battle, the police got eight of the men. One of the villains — Franny Daniels — escaped by clinging to the underside of a police van, eventually falling off when it stopped outside a West London police station. Daniels crawled away into the night. There was insufficient evidence to incriminate Spot.

One morning in late 1949, Jack Spot went to the gates of Wandsworth gaol to meet a released prisoner. It was Billy Hill, now middle aged. Once a major gangster, he had of late fallen on hard times.

Billy Hill was born in 1911 in Seven Dials, on the north side of Covent Garden. It was not then a fashionable area, but a rookery of the poor and criminal. His mother was a "buyer of bent gear", and his father could barely pass a policeman without hitting him, a compulsion which had brought him five or six convictions. There were twenty-one children in the family. Those who survived generally turned to crime. Young Billy started his working life as a grocer's delivery boy in Camden Town, but looked upon it largely as an opportunity to feed a relative tasty information about prospective targets for burglaries. He was soon doing his own, preferring "drumming" (the wholesale ransacking of a house in its owners' absence) to "creeping" (burglary while the occupants slept). Drumming was increasingly popular among criminals; there were many new, quiet suburbs, whose occupants were out during the day, and drumming tended to be more leniently viewed by the courts than creeping.

Over the years, Hill specialized in domestic theft and smash and grab raids. When the Second World War broke out, he evaded military service and with his gang found that the confusion of war-time offered new opportunities for making easy money. He broke into post-offices and opened up safes with a custom-built giant tin-opener; the black-out meant that he went undisturbed, and a depleted police force lacked the man-power to keep tabs on him. Though Hill was overtly as proud as the next man to be British, and talked of the war-time camaraderie, he became an important figure in the vast spiv-ridden world of the black market, selling stolen goods and ration cards, and keeping the well-heeled supplied with everything from petrol and nylons to fresh salmon and bacon.

The profits were huge. Hill was making £3,000 a week from burglaries and many times that from his black-market activities. He never went on the town without a "monkey" (£500) or a "grand" (£1,000) in his pocket. He wore forty-guinea Savile Row suits, silk shirts and hand-made shoes.

Though not yet an ally of Spot's, Hill was also involved in the violent demise of the White gang. Shortly afterwards he was nicked by the police. Hill had spent nearly 15 years inside, and objected to being imprisoned for a crime of which he claimed to be wholly innocent. He was indignant, and on bail decided to leave England. Pretending to be a policeman, he relieved a pair of crooks of their haul of parachute silk, and with the proceeds headed for South Africa. In Johannesburg he opened a gambling club. But he was soon involved in a battle with Arnold Neville, the emperor of South African crime. Neville was found in a pool of blood outside a night-club. He had been sliced from head to toe with razors, and needed over a hundred stitches. Hill was arrested, but his polite demeanour and respectable appearance earned him a light sentence. Afraid of extradition, he jumped bail and headed back to England. But he was sick of running, and finally gave himself up and went to Wandsworth gaol.

When Spot took Hill under his wing, it was not for altruistic reasons but because Spot's roster of trusted lieutenants had been depleted by injury and police action. Hill was a useful man, and Spot put him in charge of the spielers. He could be a cold, hard man, and it was said that his eyes were like "black glass". He was an excellent gambler, and tolerated no trouble in the clubs he ran, though his propensity for violence elsewhere often caused Spot embarrassment. Hill fell for the charms of Gypsy Riley, a tempestuous temptress and noted good-time girl. When her ex-pimp, "Belgian Johnny", tried to put her back on the game, Hill marched into a restaurant where Johnny was eating with his Belgian friends and publicly slashed his face to shreds. Spot had to work hard to persuade the Belgian to keep his mouth shut.

Spot had married a young Irish girl named Rita, and in 1951 he planned to retire. But he could not wholly trust his chief henchmen to preserve peace in the underworld and in the end he worked out a power-sharing arrangement with Hill where the latter had control of the spielers while Spot kept a firm grasp on the race-track.

But the world of gambling was changing. The Betting and Gaming Act of 1960 would legalize many of the illicit areas which the gangsters derived their wealth from. In the run-up to it, the race-course authorities went about cleaning up the activities on the courses, licensing and policing the bookmakers themselves. By the mid-1950s Spot had lost much of his authority. His less scrupulous partner was looking for opportunities to expand.

Hill had grown up when the legal system only meted out modest sentences for petty crime and theft. Such stints were regarded as an occupational hazard. The Criminal Justice Act of 1948 changed his attitude. Now he and others like him were to be regarded as "continual reoffenders", and would face longer and longer spells in jail. Hence, the rewards from petty burglary and shifting bent gear no longer justified the potential penalties. He cast around for bigger and bigger "project" crimes. In his autobiography he as good as boasted that he was responsible for the 1952 mailbag robbery, in which £287,000 in used notes – a

Billy Hill found an unlikely ally in the crusading journalist Duncan Webb, who described Hill as "a crook, a villain, a thief, a thug", but also "a genius and a kind and tolerant man". It was Webb who wrote a series of exposés for *The People* which brought about the demise of the Messina brothers, who had taken over running London's prostitution rackets. Of mixed Egyptian, Sicilian and Maltese descent, the Messina brothers ran an efficient operation in which their women worked strictly regulated hours and were limited to ten minutes per customer. One prostitute reckoned that between 1940 and 1955 she earned £150,000 for the gang; on VE Day she got through forty-nine clients. In the course of his investigations, Webb was constantly threatened by the Messina thugs. Then he met Hill, got on amicably and thereafter enjoyed the freedom of the underworld that so fascinated him. In return Webb ensured that Hill had a favourable press and even ghosted his autobiography called, with typical modesty, *Boss of Britain's Underworld*.

massive sum in those days – was stolen from post office vans ambushed between Paddington Station and the sorting office in the City. The following year a lorry carrying £45,000 in gold bullion on behalf of KLM Airways was hijacked in Holborn. Hill never had to worry about money again.

Despite dallying with retirement, Hill still took violence seriously, and in 1953 nearly got into serious trouble when he viciously chived a young East End tearaway called

Tommy Smithson, who had given offence to his beloved Gypsy. That same year Spot and Hill met two young, polite and promising lads from the East End, Ronald and Reginald Kray. The twins later said that they never had much time for Spot, but Hill certainly aided their rise to prominence.

In 1954, Hill had the nerve to begin serializing his memoirs for *The People*. The first episode blatantly explained how the KLM bullion hijack had been executed. In the ensuing public outcry, Hill decided to emigrate to Australia. When he got there he was sent straight back. Spot was, as he put it, "well pissed off" with Hill's high profile and his claims to be the emperor of crime. They fell out, and Spot, who blamed Webb for fostering Hill's delusions of grandeur, personally put on his favourite knuckleduster and beat up the journalist. The subsequent court case did nothing for his public image, and when he too tried to serialize his memoirs, they received scant attention.

By 1955, Spot was losing what little influence he still had on the racecourses to a bunch of Italian bookies and their strong-men. It was at this time that the Krays saw him again at Epsom races, at his invitation; they were happy to be noticed but decided that they would ultimately be wrong to ally themselves with such a spent force. Hill had returned from his abortive attempt to emigrate, and at that same Epsom race meeting publicly allied himself with the Italians. Soon afterwards, Spot was strolling through Frith Street in Soho when he came across Albert Dimes, a genial Italian, whom Hill had employed as a bodyguard. They began brawling outside the Bar Italia. Spot clouted Dimes on the chin. Dimes fled and tried to hide in a greengrocers shop. Spot, his temper up, seized a potato knife and stabbed Dimes with it several times before the proprietor of the shop, a formidable woman called Mrs Hyams, hit him over the head with a scoop from a set of scales. As he lay stunned, Dimes retaliated and slashed wildly at him with his knife. In the end, both men staggered off, cut to shreds. Although badly injured, they survived. But as Spot lay in hospital, the last vestiges of his criminal empire vanished.

He also ended up in court, charged with instigating the affray. Though he was acquitted, it subsequently came to light (largely as a result of work by Duncan Webb egged on by Billy Hill) that Spot's principal witness in his defence, an old and genteel clergyman called Parson Andrews, was popularly known as the "knocking Parson". Though he had a sanctimonious exterior he habitually swindled bookies and his ecclesiastical career had been devoted to whisky, gambling and women. This decrepit character had been recruited by Spot as a witness, and he and a coterie of Spot's associates and his wife Rita were eventually charged with conspiracy to pervert the course of justice. The case went badly for Spot, and this and a subsequent perjury case involving another witness ruined him.

Hill always kicked a man when he was down. One night in May, Spot and his wife Rita were strolling back to their flat in Hyde Park Mansions when they were set upon by a large group of men armed with razors, knives and coshes. Spot knew what was coming and tried to get his wife inside the door to the flats, but she refused and clung to him, screaming. Together they fell to the floor, and the men closed in on them. Rita was not cut, but Spot had seventy-eight stitches and a blood transfusion. He considered breaking the underworld code and revealing the identity of his attackers, but in the end decided not to. Although they had no respect for him, the Kray twins were looking for an opportunity to whip up a gang war in which they could assert themselves by brute force on the world of the West End, at that time still closed to them. They visited Spot in hospital, and urged him to let them start shedding blood in revenge. But such rash conflicts were anathema to Spot, and he said nothing in reply, but rolled over in his bed and faced the wall.

Rita had no qualms about talking to the law and took her husband's assailants to court. In the end, three of Hill's henchmen went to jail.

In the aftermath of the endless trials, Jack Spot was finally declared bankrupt and evicted from his Bayswater flat. Rita made a little pile of money from selling her life story and opened the Highball Club, which quickly became a popular haunt for the glitterati. But Hill didn't want Spot around in any form, and the club was constantly plagued by fires and pointless vandalism. Spot gave up and emigrated. He wanted to go to Canada, but when he was refused admission he settled for Ireland. Here he retreated into comfortable obscurity, working as a bookie's runner in Dublin and Cork. His marriage survived and his daughters went into show-business. Later, he returned to England, and lived a quiet life, making occasional appearances as a celebrity at sporting events.

Hill also assumed a lower profile, bought a villa in Marbella and delegated the handling of many of his affairs. Many of his gang drifted off to join the Richardson gang from South London, and became involved in the subsequent dispute with the Krays. Throughout the sixties Hill enjoyed a period of prosperity and respectability. He became close to the Kray twins, to whom he was invaluable as a guide to the low-life of London's West End and Soho. He was friends with journalists other than Duncan Webb and the rising media personalities of the era. He hob-nobbed with nobility, and gambled with Perac Rachman and Mandy Rice-Davies. Based for the most part in Spain, he was far removed from the unfavourable Kray-instigated scandals of the London underworld in the 1960s.

In the early 1970s he got fed up and returned to England, opening a night-club in Sunningdale. In 1976 he split up with his long-standing moll, Gypsy, and took up with a black singer, with whom, to his surprise, he fell deeply in love. It was late in the day to discover such tender feelings, and when, three years later, she committed suicide, Hill sank into depression and misanthropy and shut himself up in his flat. He was cursed to live until 1984, and died a lonely and unhappy man. Jack Spot described him as "the richest man in the graveyard".

Chapter Eleven

"JUNGLE W11": RACHMAN AND MICHAEL X

"Jungle W11" was the name the London police gave to the Notting Hill area of West London in the 1950s. Now gentrified and hugely fashionable, the haunt of publishers, journalists, actors and the like, the area was once considerably run-down and seedy. The Notting Hill police station area stretched from the expensive genteel houses off Notting Hill Gate and Holland Park to the large, run-down and overcrowded properties of North Kensington and Paddington. In the poorer areas settled the West Indian immigrant population. The proximity of the area to the West End and the fact that at that time street prostitution extended from Marble Arch, all along the Bayswater Road, to Shepherds Bush, meant that the crumbling properties of Notting Hill had become coveted bases for organized operators in the field of vice. Illegal drinking clubs and rip-off joints were widespread, and the area was a bastion of the drug trade.

The immigrant West Indian community was easy prey for racketeering landlords, most notably Perac Rachman, whose name has become synonymous with rent extortion: "Rachmanism" is now in the dictionary.

Perac Rachman was born in Poland in 1920 and came to England as a penniless refugee in the wake of the Second World War; by the time he died in 1962, aged only forty-two, he was a millionaire.

Gangsters

When he arrived in London he started off by doing casual work in the East End, then obtaining a job as a clerk at an estate agent's office in Shepherds Bush, a little further west than Notting Hill. The 1957 Rent Act made it possible for landlords to charge much higher rents than those hitherto paid by existing sitting tenants whose low rents were legally protected. However, Rachman had an astute mind and saw that the new Rent Act, the severe post-war shortage of housing, and the influx of immigrants desperate for accommodation offered a considerable opportunity to make money. The immigrants were a particularly vulnerable group; they had arrived in Britain to find that there was little rented accommodation available and that they were a low priority for council housing. Ignorant of the laws of the country, they would take whatever accommodation they were offered.

Rachman began to buy up large Victorian terraced properties, often on short leases, in North Kensington and Paddington. He obtained the capital principally from the Eagle Star Building Society, which in 1957 lent Rachman nearly sixty per cent of its total loans for the year, amounting to nearly £60,000; by the end of 1959 the company had lent Rachman and his associated companies – the police identified about thirty-three of which he was director and principal shareholder – over £220,000. The extent of the society's involvement was not discovered until much later, as none of Rachman's concerns was lent more than £25,000 and only details of the loans above this figure had to be disclosed in the society's annual returns.

Having purchased a property, Rachman's first move was to get rid of its existing sitting tenants. Initially he would offer them a modest pay-off to quit. If that was refused, life would become unpleasant for the tenants. Rachman would install some of his trusted henchmen in adjoining rooms, and suggest that they have a few all-night parties, turn the music up as loud as possible, let rubbish pile up in the communal areas and generally make living conditions as intolerable as possible for the existing tenants. If they still refused to go, strong-arm men would cut off the water and electrical supplies, smash up communal toilets and remove the external locks to the house, leaving it unsafe. The tenants would be left in no doubt that physical violence would follow.

Some courageous tenants did take their cases to local rent tribunals or considered legal action, but the majority tended to be poor people, for whom the complexities of civil law were a mystery. Furthermore, it was impossible to find direct evidence linking Rachman to the intimidation. Most sitting tenants quit their flats. Rachman then sent in the cowboy builders, subdivided the flats still further, made a few cosmetic repairs and re-let the accommodation at a still higher rent, either to immigrant families or to prostitutes looking for working space.

Rachman was living in a vast house in the exclusive area of Hampstead. He had a full time domestic staff, and was chauffeured around London in a Rolls-Royce, while his poverty-stricken tenants were crammed together in squalid, tiny flats, their exorbitant rents collected by men who had little time for excuses and quickly resorted to physical intimidation. A short, podgy, bespectacled and prematurely balding individual, he hardly looked like an emperor of crime and had a rather incongruous reputation as a ladies' man.

By 1959, allegations about Rachman's often violent methods were beginning to trouble the authorities, but since he avoided personal contact with tenants, it seemed impossible to mount a sustainable case against him. His financial affairs were targeted; his companies certainly owed tax, and a prosecution by the Inland Revenue would have forced him into bankruptcy. But, as his companies' shares had only a nominal face value, sometimes of a few pounds, it would have done him little damage. As much of his

Michael X

accommodation was let to prostitutes the police tried to get a conviction for brothel-keeping and living on the earnings of prostitutes, but could not gather sufficient evidence; Rachman was a cunning operator. The police tried again, and came sufficiently close to rattle Rachman. He sold his Notting Hill interests, and kept a low profile until his death three years later.

Rachman employed some of London's seediest types as enforcers. Among them were Raymond Nash, a Lebanese who later developed an interest in Soho's clubs and was finally barred from Britain after a conviction abroad for smuggling gold, and George Pigott, a well-known armed robber, currently serving a life sentence for his alleged involvement in the contract killing of "Italian Toni" Zomparelli, who was blown away in a Soho amusement arcade in 1974.

The most infamous of Rachman's henchmen was Michael Campbell De Freitas, a Trinidadian, who later reinvented himself as a black-power leader in the style of Malcolm X, and called himself Michael X. During the 1960s he acted as an agent for Rachman in the now prestigious areas of Colville Terrace and Powis Square in Notting Hill. He was heavily involved in a number of vice rackets, and for the right money arranged working accommodation for prostitutes. He was convicted for keeping a brothel, but though he had a fearsome reputation as a pimp and extortionist, he got off with a conditional discharge and a nominal fine.

Inspired by Malcolm X, he then became a Muslim, going under the name of Abdul Malik, later Michael X. He founded the "Racial Adjustment Action Society", and became the self-appointed Messiah of a black-power commune on the grimy Holloway Road in Islington, North London. De Freitas attracted a number of wealthy and influential followers, and found himself a hit with young, middle class white women, notably the ill-starred Gale Benson, daughter of the Conservative MP for Chatham.

Gangsters

The enthusiasm of his followers did not wane when he was imprisoned for twelve months after publicly urging the shooting of any black girl seen with a white man.

His organized criminal activities continued throughout his immoderate political career. In 1969, De Freitas and four of his associates were put on trial at the Old Bailey, accused of robbery and demanding money with menaces. The proprietor of an employment agency in Soho had been subject to extortion, and when he had expressed a reluctance to pay, De Freitas had put a dog collar on his neck and forced him to crawl around the floor, begging for mercy.

De Freitas jumped bail and headed back to Trinidad, where he was followed by some of his supporters, including Gale Benson. There De Freitas formed a black-power party, and joined up with local criminals, creating a gang that was to prove a constant source of fury to the authorities. In 1972, a member of the gang, a man called Joseph Skerritt, refused to obey De Freitas's orders and carry out a raid on a local police station. De Freitas announced to his gang that he needed to improve the drainage in his garden, and ordered a number of them, including Skerritt, to dig a long trench. When this was done, De Freitas decapitated Skerritt with a cutlass and threw him into the trench. The other members of his gang became worried about their esteemed leader's erratic behaviour, and with good reason. Shortly afterwards, another of their number mysteriously drowned, and Gale Benson vanished. When De Freitas and his wife went away on a lecture tour, one of his henchmen set fire to his bungalow. While investigating the arson, a police inspector rooted around De Freitas's garden and became suspicious of some abnormally tall and horribly yellow lettuces. They began digging, and soon found the corpse of Skerritt. Two days later, Gale Benson's body was found, five foot underground. The pathologist deduced that she had been stabbed with a six-inch blade, but that it had not killed her outright. She had been buried alive.

Two of De Freitas's gang were convicted and hanged for her murder. Though De Freitas himself was indicted for the murder of Gale Benson, he was never tried for the crime. Convicted of the murder of Skerritt, he went to the gallows in 1974.

Chapter Twelve

DRUG BARONS

O utside the Mafia, the international drugs trade is often controlled at its roots by a series of powerful individuals, drug barons, whose power base is the source of production within often lawless and poor countries, much of whose gross national income is connected to narcotics.

Colombia's economy has for many years depended largely on the export of cocaine; at one stage it was estimated that Colombia was exporting something like 100 tons of cocaine annually with a street value in excess of sixty billion dollars, representing forty per cent of the country's gross national product. With no alternative source of revenue in the impoverished and mountainous rural areas, government attempts to tackle the problem have met with stiff and violent local resistance; the impetus to drive out the drug producers has come largely from America, which has offered military training, equipment and financial incentives to the South American governments.

Trafficking in Colombia has long been controlled by a few powerful and wealthy dynasties. In the drug capitals of Medellin and Cali live the families of Escobar, Lehder, O'Campo and Ochoa, who have run the country with the liberal use of graft and the gun. One of the most prominent of these families is the Escobar clan. It has been claimed that Pablo Escobar, its head, a man in his early forties, is among the ten richest individuals in the world. Based in Medellin, where he runs five homes, Escobar's official status as a wanted man has done little to persuade him to keep a low profile. A public benefactor, his grandiose gifts to the poor – including building thousands of new homes – have given him the status of a hero and guaranteed that the slum-dwellers and the starving of Colombia are unlikely to surrender him to the authorities. The government does not have the funds to match the generosity of the criminals, and those politicians who refuse to be bought are murdered with impunity. In Medellin, a comparatively small regional capital city of a million people, there are nearly ten murders a day, principally drug-related, the result of quarrels between cartels, or of the enforcement of drug-law. In Colombia, it is quite customary for a cartel to kill not only an offender, but his entire family. In such surroundings of grinding poverty human life is seen as cheap.

Although Colombia is the leading exporter of cocaine, much of its output is actually grown elsewhere in South America, with Colombia forming a centre for refinement and distribution. Bolivia and its own drug baron, Roberto Suarez, are responsible for a substantial slice of the actual coca crop from which the cocaine is extracted. Suarez is unusual in that, far from being a gangster who has struggled out of the gutter, he is an educated and affluent man from a rich family. Once a cattle rancher, he discovered that his remote land holdings in the regions around Beni, Chapare and Santa Cruz could be far more profitably used for growing the stunted, wiry coca bushes.

Possessing an annual income in the region of one billion dollars, Suarez acquired a favourable public image in the accepted fashion, buying the hearts of the poor with lavish beneficence, building roads, schools and hospitals. Suarez was alleged to have had his own private army, the so-called "Fiances of Death", whose leader was reputed to be a mild-mannered German who went under the name of Klauss Altmann, better known to the world as the one-time Gestapo officer, Klaus Barbie, the "Butcher of Lyon", a resident of Bolivia since 1951.

After decades of de facto rule, the drug barons of Bolivia
were disconcerted when, in 1978, the country democrati-
cally elected Silus Zuazo to the position of president. His
predecessor, Hugo Banzer, had been a substantial trafficker
in his own right, but Zuazo promised the Americans he
would take on the cocaine kings. It was unlikely that he
would have much effect, but to guarantee his failure, Suarez
instigated a military coup led by disaffected officers eager
for power and money. Colonel Luis Arce Gomez (a cousin
of Suarez) was paid $800,000 to effect the necessary
introductions, and General Luis Garcia Meza, head of the
armed forces and the leader of the insurgency – the 189th
coup in the short history of the Bolivian state – received a
sum well in excess of one million dollars as a down payment
on his future cut of the action. The coup, on 17 July 1980,
was a success and Suarez became the effective ruler of
Bolivia; his paid killers worked openly alongside the armed
forces to suppress and exterminate civil opposition. Within
two weeks of the takeover, 500 civilians had died, and
several thousand more were imprisoned and subject to
beatings and torture. Such authority also gave Suarez
licence to break up and absorb the smaller rival cocaine
cartels throughout Bolivia.

Meza's brutal and corrupt regime devastated the already
tottering legitimate economy. The dictates of the International Monetary Fund were wholly ignored, inflation
reached three figures and the United States suspended all
aid. Perturbed by the bad reputation his nation was acquir-
ing, and fearful of military intervention by the United States,
Suarez encouraged Meza to mount a suitable weak, cosmetic
and stage-managed campaign against a few minor cartels. It
was enough to silence the Americans temporarily. Within
the year, however, Suarez, the puppet-master of Bolivian
politics, decided to bestow the crown of the bungling Meza
elsewhere. In September 1981, he engineered yet another
coup and replaced Meza with General Torrelio Villa, who in

turn was discarded in favour of General Guido Calderon, who made the usual promises of democratic elections.

Suarez profited while Bolivia went to ruin. Finally, in the face of public unrest, Calderon was forced out of office and Zuazo returned from exile to confront the mess: a nation with no industry, massive unemployment and the highest murder rate in the world. Zuazo did good things. He deported Klaus Barbie back to Europe to face trial; he purged the army and put Gomez, Meza and a host of others to flight. But the problems of cocaine growing required dealing with at a fundamentally economic level; the poor farmers had to be financially encouraged to grow something other than coca. He turned to the Americans for help, and they created the crop substitution programme, offering forty million dollars in subsidies to farmers prepared to renounce coca in favour of legitimate crops. But no crop has such a good profit margin, and once the subsidy is accepted there is little way, in the mountainous terrain of Bolivia, to ensure that the farmers actually switch crops. For the past decade the authorities have fought an increasingly bitter battle against the cocaine barons, with only a small degree of success.

For a long time, cocaine was not seen as a major problem in the same way as heroin. It was a social drug. "Cocaine" said one American "is God's way of telling you that you're too rich". That was once true; the cocaine economy depended upon the criminal manipulation of a wealthy First World, for whom cocaine was the consumer drug *par excellence*, and the poverty of the Third World, where conditions allowed unfettered production. The rich got their kicks, the poor made a living and the organizers were as wealthy as Croesus. But the over-production of cocaine by the greedy South American barons led to an excess on the streets; not even the huge white middle class of America could snort all that powder. With the street price plummeting, it was necessary to make the cocaine accessible to the huge market of the vast underclass; to put it in competition with heroin. Crack – the drug of poverty and of violent escape – was created.

The traditional source of heroin is the Golden Triangle, 80,000 square miles of mountainous jungle at the point where Thailand, Laos and Burma intersect. Bounded by the Mekong and Mae Si Rivers, it is virtually impassable except to the native inhabitants, the Shan, the mountain people. It is unpoliceable terrain.

The Shan, in turn, feel little allegiance to the three national powers that hold sway over the territory. Theirs is still a feudal society, and their lords are individuals like Khun Sa, the world's biggest opium producer. The son of a former Colonel in Chiang Kai Shek's Chinese Nationalist army, Khun Sa's power stems from the vagaries of American foreign policy in Asia. When the Nationalist army was defeated and driven into Burma by the Communists, it remained largely intact and was welcomed first by the Shan tribesmen as a buffer against the local government in Rangoon, and then by the Americans, who saw the continued presence of the exiled Nationalists in Burma as a bulwark against the spread of Communism. The Americans kept them supplied with arms and money for more than a decade.

In the late 1950s, the Burmese government, hitherto tolerant of the Nationalist presence, decided that they were now too powerful, and pushed them out towards Thailand and Laos. The Americans gradually cut off the flow of aid, although covertly the CIA continued to support them for another fifteen years. But, with their sources of revenue seriously disrupted, the Nationalists began to look for alternative income, and moved into the cultivation of opium poppies, which have for centuries been a staple cash crop of the region, a situation largely ignored by the Burmese government.

Hong Kong policemen lead away some of the 800 men suspected members of "Triads"

Young Khun Sa grew up to become the Nationalists' main link with the CIA, supplying them with information about Communist insurgency while exporting massive amounts of heroin to the USA. The situation was entirely hypocritical; the American administration was openly at war with Khun Sa and his compatriots while their principal intelligence organ was employing him as an agent. During the Vietnam War, as many as one in seven American soldiers took heroin, probably supplied by Khun Sa, the same man who the CIA regarded as an ally. The American soldiers disliked the coarse, brown, smoking heroin the locals used and Khun Sa obligingly turned to manufacturing heroin in the form of a fine white powder suitable for intravenous injection.

In the 1970s, Khun Sa expanded his operations, encouraging Thai farmers to increase their output of raw opium base, and began to ship heroin to Bangkok, where he had formed a link with the Triads, Chinese gangsters.

When the American servicemen went home, Khun Sa began dumping his stocks on the streets of America's cities. His profits were enormous; a kilo of raw opium base costing $3,000 at source could fetch up to three million on the streets. The operation was run with corporate efficiency and Khun Sa had his hooks in most of the authorities; the Thai police have even been known to run some of his heroin manufacturing laboratories. In 1978 he even had the nerve to propose to the American Government that they could solve the nation's heroin problems by buying 500 tons of opium base a year off him, at a cost of fifty million dollars; but the Americans decided that he had sufficient supplies to sell this to them and still flood the streets.

In 1980, the Americans put a price of $25,000 on his head and furiously urged the Thai authorities to do something about his activities. In 1982 they finally did, launching a huge, American-sponsored assault on his hilltop fortress at Ban Hin Taek, a small Thai mountain village. The attack force of 2,000 troops supported by helicopter gunships killed over 200 of Khun Sa's private army and captured ten tons of weapons, but the mastermind was gone. He and the bulk of his forces slipped across the border into Burma where he immediately went into the heroin business with Communist insurgents. Two years later, he returned to Ban Hin Taek, and there he has remained; the Thai government has now become quite desperate in its struggle against the drug traffickers – one in fifty of its own population is an addict – and customarily awards the death penalty for trafficking. But the Golden Triangle remains impossible to police and the Shan tribes are still adamantly uncooperative. A quarter of them use the drug and all of them rely on it financially. To stop the heroin, and oust Khun Sa, would require a bloody war or an aid programme of monumental proportions.